PERSONAL
STYLE

PERSONAL STYLE

by
James Wagenvoord

Illustrations by Sandra Forrest

Foreword by
GEOFFREY BEENE

HOLT, RINEHART AND WINSTON

NEW YORK

For Linda Raglan Cunningham

Published by Holt, Rinehart and Winston,
383 Madison Avenue, New York, New York, 10017
Published simultaneously in Canada by Holt, Rinehart
and Winston of Canada, Limited

Library of Congress Cataloging in Publication Data
Wagenvoord, James.
Personal style.
1. Executives—Conduct of life.   I. Title.
HD38.2.W34   1985   658.4'094   85–14075
ISBN 0-03-004068-X

First Edition
Printed in the United States of America
1   3   5   7   9   10   8   6   4   2

ISBN 0-03-004068-X

ACKNOWLEDGMENTS

I am grateful to the many people who gave me their time and their insight during the making of *Personal Style*, particularly Thomas E. Moloney III, who has been this book's driving force since its beginning.

Special thanks also go to Helen Anderson, Aimee Lee Ball, Frank Barbuscio, G. Douglas Burck, John Cadenhead, Thomas Conway, Ralph DiNapoli, Teddy Donifrio, Ronald Dunton, Diana Espino, Shelly Fireman, Frank Giambrone, Judith Goldberg, Michael Goldenberg, Leslie Grunberg, Leona Helmsley, Nora Holley, Justin Hoy, James Hunt, Frank Hurd, Jay Jacobs, Ken Johnson, Scott Kale, Pat Keller, Robert Kelly, Henry Lambert, David Larkin, Maurice Mann, Jean-Claude Nédélec, Alan Parter, Jane Pasanen, Nan Puryear, Sabina Roth, Carl Ruff, Nancy Ruiz, Vincent Sardi, Phil Scotty, Mimi Sheraton, Lucio Sorre, Gale Stoppert, Carlton Thompson, Carm Tintle, Mort Todel, Liz Trotta, Laurence Tucci, Stanley Tucker, Allan Wahler, Bernice Wiseman, Marian Wood, Barry Yarkon.

FOREWORD

Style is an expression of personal identity. And arriving at your personal style is a very complex process, filled with trial and error. I've always compared it to designing—my designs look very simple, but achieving that simplicity is extremely complex.

Personal style extends into whatever a man does. Whether he is relaxing during the weekend or attending a board meeting, that style should always be evident. The choices made by a man with his own personal style work in any situation. It is his signature.

Personal style does not require dressing in a bizarre or unorthodox fashion, although that approach works well for some men (Tom Wolfe is one example; Mick Jagger is another). For most of us, the drama is not that necessary. It happens in stages. And it takes a long time to develop. It evolves as a man listens to himself. It's courageous and adventuresome, in a very real sense.

I feel strongly that clothes should not be worn competitively. They should be worn because you enjoy them and you feel good in them. It's much more meaningful to dress as an individual than to be a mirror image of everyone else. The clothes are not wearing you, you're wearing them.

And there's a certain ease when you're not concerned with what you're wearing. That's something I personally strive for—I think this sense of ease will be a great concern for designers who are concerned with the future.

Individualism makes a man stand out. As a designer, I simply
suggest to men what they should wear and I design the clothes
accordingly. I'm always delighted when a design leaves my hands,
moves into the store, and onto a man's back. It ceases to be mine. It
becomes the personal statement of the individual—how he wears
it and puts it together. And that is most gratifying. It's not a dictate
(I don't think anything should be, because what's good for one is
not good for another). My role is simply a matter of aiding the man,
of trying to make it a little easier for him.

There's a great difference between style and fashion. Fashion is
what you buy; style is how you wear it. Being fashionable means
unflinchingly accepting direction, following the trends, and
focusing upon what's "in" at the moment—this year or this season.
Personal style, however, is something that endures. It is self-
directed and it is the result of making distinct choices—accepting
what is good and rejecting what you feel is not for you. In the sense
of being trendy or changing, style has little to do with fashion. The
constant within fashion is that of flux. There is, however, a
consistency, a substance, to style. And it includes your intellect and
your sensitivity, and what you can and cannot accomplish. And as
style is developed you reach a point where, without any
self-consciousness, you're basically in control of the situation.

—GEOFFREY BEENE
New York, 1985

CONTENTS

PERSONAL STYLE

PERSONAL STYLE. It shouldn't be surprising that the French have a phrase for it, "Etre bien dans sa peau." They seem to have a word or a phrase to sum up just about anything and everything. It means to fit well within one's skin—to be comfortable within yourself. It means being relaxed enough to get on with the job at hand, free of worrisome distractions about form and fashion. And it means being sure enough of yourself to make a personal statement to the world: "This is who I am, this is what you get."

Substance and style, as personal social identity, are a complex matter. Things that work for one individual don't necessarily work for another. Yet through this very complexity one arrives at the simplest form and shape. It's just that the process of arriving at simplicity is an involved journey. For most of us it is a process of trial and error, of deciding what feels right and what doesn't. You must be honest with yourself in order to critically view your good and bad points. And play them up or down accordingly.

Personal style goes far beyond the media myths. The modern lovers who shine out at us from films and television screens are, with very few exceptions, the owners of chiseled profiles, boyishly winsome or brooding faces, and trimly shaped forms. But in the real day-after-day world there are many people who couldn't handle screen tests but do very well on their own terms by looking and acting comfortably like themselves. It is a very good look. If you were to ask what a great lover should look like, the answer could be "a short man, considerable girth, grey hair, terribly nearsighted, thick glasses, and knock knees." The name's Onassis. Admittedly, owning a lot of super tankers didn't handicap him, but neither was it the reason for the answer. Liz Trotta, a correspondent for CBS News, tells a story of a Sunday in New York City.

"It was a Sunday-afternoon brunch at P.J. Clarke's. I was with two other women, and the three of us were very dressed and looking very young New York career girl-ish. The place was jammed, and in the middle of all this a short, stout man, stocky really, walked in. I thought he looked familiar. I was facing the door, so I got a good look at him. All of a sudden I realized that it was Aristotle Onassis. I let my friends know, but very carefully, because, like most New Yorkers, I had learned not to disturb someone's privacy. Everybody in the place knew who he was within two minutes. Nobody stared, nobody went up to him and said something silly. He sat down at a table completely by himself, now facing the three of us. And everybody was sort of pretending that they didn't know that Aristotle Onassis was there, but very much aware of it. I was struck by—really, his personal magnetism. He had nice clothes on, but nothing you would rave about. He was wearing a blue blazer, a kind of country outfit, but very magnetic, very much a presence. He stared at the three of us.

Unlike most American men, who avoid your eyes, he really looked at us. He looked at us openly and with a kind of pleased admiration. He just enjoyed looking at three women all dressed up. It wasn't intimidating—it was flattering. One had the feeling that he liked women, not just coveted them or chased them, but he really liked women. He was soon joined by another man. And I overheard part of the conversation. They were talking about where they got their ties, like any two guys. They each had a hamburger and we left them there. But there was no doubt that he was something to look at— you could feel that he was a presence."

Perhaps one of the occasions when personal style comes under the most intense scrutiny is when a member of an executive search firm—or "headhunter"—reaches the stage of meeting a prospective candidate in person. By this time, experience, education, age, income level—factors that define the professional parameters— have been defined and the "fit" has been made. According to Carlton Thompson, managing director of Spencer Stewart Associates, one of the country's leading executive recruiters, "The purpose of the first meeting is to get a snapshot in your head and then, and only then, to get more specific about professional or business performance, the highlights—how someone did what he did, and why he is valuable.

"In its widest possible sense, however, a man's Self is the sum total of all that he can call his, not only his body and his psychic powers, but his clothes and his house, his wife and children, his ancestors and friends, his reputation and works, his lands and horses, and yacht and bank account."
—WILLIAM JAMES

"The real test is a combination of a lot of things. Is he fit, attractive? Does he take care of himself? Does he need a haircut? Is he pale or healthy looking? Handshake—some people are a big disappointment—out comes the hand and it's a big handful of mush. Does the person project? Is there life there, enthusiasm, energy, a sense of himself? Sometimes there's too much—the man just can't wait to tell you how great he is. There's too much preparation. Nobody looks that good. Doesn't he work? Doesn't he get rumpled, like me? There's too much gold, too much scent. It brings up other questions. Is he too self-centered? What's he trying to say? It's distracting.

13

"Clothing is part of it. It doesn't have to be Brooks Brothers or Burberry, but it should be attractive and well stated, not overstated. You know—is the suit threadbare? Are the shoes shined? Are the socks over the calf or wadded around the ankles?

"Regardless of the specific job or function we're seeking to fill we have to imagine this person joining the client's organization and being invited to meet the board of directors. You picture the door opening; the candidate comes in, and the board collectively thinks, 'that man has something worth listening to,' or says, 'oh, my God.'"

Achieving a comfortable syle is a rewarding experience. For you can rid yourself of the distractions of being jarringly out of step and relax and get on with your work, or you can just relax. You can *enjoy* clothing rather than being concerned about it. And grooming. And social interaction. And being comfortable. Clearly there are several things that all those Frenchmen aren't wrong about.

GROOMING

The introduction to grooming, for most men, takes place some-where between the twelfth and fourteenth birthdays. Around that time, he has mustered enough thin facial hair to justify his first shave. Looking back, it seems as though the tools of shaving simply appeared: a safety razor, a can of mentholated shaving cream, a bottle of aftershave (which seemed to set the face on fire) and, to complete the ritual, a bottle of cologne with a scent strong enough that, had he used it more than once, would have allowed him to be tracked, weeks later, by a hound with a failing memory. Soap? He had been using soap—whatever kind appeared on the bathroom sink—since he had reached school age. Deodorant? Whatever brand found in the medicine chest was good enough. Talc? That wasn't for grown-ups. It was baby powder.

From that beginning, the pattern takes shape. Keep your hair clean and dandruff-free, wash your face, and shave every morning—un-less you can find a reason to spend a day or two with stubble—spray on that deodorant, and take on the world.

For most men, it hasn't changed much. Grooming, to the uninitiated, remains a chore. But that need not be the case. There's much more to it—and you can have a good time doing it.

THE GROOMING SEQUENCE

Internationally recognized men's grooming expert Scott Kale conducts seminars attended by salespeople from leading department stores throughout the country. At the heart of Kale's message is the following eight-step daily regimen that includes subtly fragranced grooming products. It takes about twenty minutes to complete, and it works. The look that results from consistent use of the sequence is terrific.

"To be totally groomed a man should brush his teeth, shower, wash and dry his hair, shave, wash his face with the 'splash technique' which is detailed later, apply aftershave, and then moisturize the face and neck. Add some deodorant, talc, and cologne and he's set for the day.

MEN'S FRAGRANCES

"A fragrance can echo your mood or serve as your signature. Fragrances, in the form of colognes, aftershave lotions, aftershave balms, scented skin conditioners, and even scented soaps and talc can be an important part of any man's wardrobe. If you don't generally wear a fragrance, it may take a little time to find the one that suits you best.

GEOFFREY BEENE

"Men have to learn to stay with the same fragrance throughout the grooming sequence. A pine scented shampoo followed by a menthol shaving cream and a spicy aftershave is going to result in a mixture of scents that that will fight each other, killing any effect you're trying to create. Decide which kind of fragrance you prefer, then use it across the board, for everything from soap to shampoo to deodorants.

"Although there are hundreds of fragrances available, they all belong to at least one of three general scent categories: *green*, a woody, floral scent which includes Grey Flannel and Halston's I12; *spicy*, which includes products such as Pierre Cardin, Aramis, and Halston's Z14; and *citrus*, which includes Eau Sauvage and Nina Ricci's Signor Ricci.

"Every fragrance is composed of three 'notes' that vary during the day. Your first impression of any cologne is called its 'top note.' This initial scent lasts only a few minutes and may bear little resemblance to the fragrance's main scent, or 'middle note,' which lasts from three to five hours. The middle note is followed by the 'dry down,' which can last up to ten hours.

"When choosing a fragrance, remember that scents interact with body chemistry. This makes a given fragrance smell differently on different people. Never simply sniff a bottle of cologne—all you'll smell will be its top note, not the fragrance's true character. To sample a cologne, rub it on your wrist and then walk around the store for ten minutes—it takes that long for the cologne to blend with your body chemistry. If you like the way it smells after ten minutes, it's a good choice for you. If you plan on sampling a few scents, try to keep them away from each other—put one on each wrist and one on the inside of each elbow, for example. If the scents blend, they'll lose their individuality and will probably smell terrible.

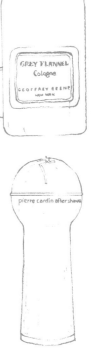

SHOWER AND SHAMPOO

"The average man will get in the shower, put shampoo on his hair, lather it up, wash and rinse the rest of his body, then rinse his hair. That, in essence, is the correct sequence. But there's more to it. What you use on your hair is critical. Unless your hair is colored or in some way chemically treated, you shouldn't follow a shampoo with a separate conditioner too often. A concentrated conditioner can make a man's relatively short hair fly away or flop in his face so that it will never show the benefit of a great cut or a great styling. A better shampoo, one that incorporates a conditioner, should be used daily. Use a combination shampoo/conditioner made with a non-soap formula. They're non-abrasive and are usually safe for color treated hair. Many of them are charged with positive and negative protein molecules that make the hair look thicker by making each shaft stand on its own. This adds bulk and volume.

"As you're finishing with your shampoo and shower—when the

lather has been rinsed from your hair and all the soap has been rinsed from your body—hold your head under the cold water and let it run through your hair for just a second. That closes the hair cuticles and makes the hair extremely shiny.

"When you're out of the shower, towel dry your hair until it is just damp, not wet. This takes about fifty shakes with a towel on your head, then it's ready for blow drying. (Don't overdry it with the towel or you won't be able to control it with the blow dryer.) It's best to put your shaving cream or foam on now and, while it is setting on your skin, you can blow dry your hair. If you have flyaway hair, mist it very lightly with hair spray before you blow it. When it's dry, you'll have a beautiful style without stiffness. Then begin the actual shaving process.

SHAVING

"Never begin the shaving process using upward strokes, which many men do. This causes nicks and cuts. First remove the bulk of the beard from your face with downward strokes. Then, very gently, stroke your throat with an upward motion. When that's done, you can begin holding the cheeks taut and shaving up and across. The greatest shaving error of all is shaving before you shower, which doesn't give the steam a chance to set up your beard.

"Men who have skin conditions—seborrhea, psoriasis, acne—should never shave with a blade. They should always use an electric razor, which won't irritate the skin as much as a safety razor will. Use talc as the pre-electric shave conditioner, not a liquid which can clog the blades and irritate an existing skin problem.

"Most men rinse their razor blades in hot water. Never do that—it dulls the blade. You'll get three times the wear out of a razor blade if you rinse it in lukewarm water instead.

"No matter what razor you use, complete your shave by rinsing your face thoroughly, then washing it with the splash technique.

"One of the greatest things a man can buy is a non-fogging shaving mirror to hang over the shower caddy. It lets you shave in the shower. You get a barber-type shave when you do that."
—MICHAEL GOLDENBERG, *men's grooming expert*

THE SPLASH TECHNIQUE

"To look its best, your skin needs both internal and external care. Excessive exposure to the sun and wind will dry and weather skin (particularly your face), making you look older than you really are. And a poor diet can make your skin prone to acne, bruising, uneven color, and flaking. Lederle Laboratories approved the splash technique, a simple face cleansing regimen for men that thoroughly purges the skin of debris and impurities. Use the splash technique twice a day. Research shows that sixty percent of American men wash their faces only in the morning, but it's important to remove the grime of the day from your face before you go to sleep if you want to keep your skin balanced and looking its best. You'll begin to see a difference in your skin's tone and texture within ten days.

"You have to begin with a soap that contains no deodorants. We recommend a pure, hard-milled soap, the kind that can be bought at men's cosmetic counters in department stores. Although the cost may appear to be high, it's actually economical. A hard-milled soap has had most traces of water removed from it and will last about eight times longer than ordinary soap.

"Before you wash your face, pull your hair back from your forehead. Use a runner's terrycloth sweatband if you have one handy. Run water that's as hot as your hands can tolerate into a clean stoppered sink until the sink is about three quarters full. Don't worry about the hot water burning your face; the face can tolerate a temperature twenty degrees higher than your hands can. Wet the bar of soap and work it into a rich lather between the palms of your hands. Massage the lather into your face and throat with the tips of your fingers, concentrating on the forehead, nose, and chin, where you have the greatest concentration of oil glands.

"Next, bend over the sink and splash your face from twenty to thirty times with the water from the sink, not running water. The soap will form an emulsion with the excretions of the skin and rebalance it, making it neither oily or dry but, in fact, perfectly balanced. Balanced skin is a rarity in the United States because we are constantly exposed to climate controlled environments.

"Don't make the mistake of rinsing your face with clear water—that will only strip the acid mantle of the skin and make it dry. And never put cold water on your face—it constricts the blood vessels and can break capillaries.

"When you've finished splashing, your skin should be bright pink. If it's not, the water was not hot enough and the technique has not been effective. Very hot water is essential to stimulate the skin's glands. If your skin is dry, the hot water will stimulate the oil glands to produce again, and in the case of an oily skin the hot water will help open the sebaceous glands and allow excess oils to flow free. Blot your face gently with a towel, leaving it slightly moist.

AFTERSHAVE

"Now apply the correct aftershave to close the pores and cleanse the tiny nicks that shaving invariably leaves in the delicate skin of the face. Shaving is very much a surgical procedure—if you look at your face under a magnifying glass when you've finished shaving, you'll see you've made tiny little breaks in the skin. The skin is the largest organ of the body, and it's there to protect the internal systems from germs. When you shave, you're creating tiny passages through which germs can enter the body. In addition to feeling refreshing, an astringent aftershave contains alcohol and will kill germs on the skin. Aftershave lotions are best for men with normal to oily skin; aftershave balm is for men with normal to dry skin. Because of the fragrance concentration in lotion and balm, they can't be applied around the eyes. They never take the place of moisturizer.

"Aftershave products can be used to refresh your skin quickly, no matter where you are. Most aftershave lotions contain astringents, which act as cleansers. Keep a spare container of aftershave lotion in your desk—if your skin feels oily during the day, apply it to your face. Your skin will look and feel cleaner.

MOISTURIZER

"The next step is to smooth on a moisturizer. If you have dry skin, apply it as a fine film to the entire face and throat (avoiding the eyes and nose); if your skin is oily, apply it only to the throat and under the eyes. By the time you've finished blending the moisturizer, your face has returned to its normal color.

"Don't use a moisturizer formulated for a woman's skin. That's meant to be used under makeup, and it will leave an unattractive shiny film on a man's face. A good man's moisturizer is made from natural ingredients, such as soothing allantoin from the comfrey plant, vitamin E, cucumber extract, and aloe vera. It will dry to a smooth, undetectable finish on the skin.

UNDERARMS

"When you put on your deodorant, don't forget talc—it's a natural absorbent. Applying talc over your deodorant makes it forty percent more effective. It's a must in warm weater. Try sprinkling talc in your running shorts to prevent chafing, and in your shoes to keep your feet and the leather dry. Avoid baby powder—it contains mica which is always bad for men's skin because the mica flakes are small enough to get into men's larger pores and clog them. Instead, look for a talc that contains cornstarch, a natural absorbent.

COLOGNE

"When you make a cologne part of your fragrance and cosmetic wardrobe, splash or spray a small amount of it onto your chest before you put your shirt on in the morning. Remember that cologne is meant to be applied anywhere from your collarbone to your toes—not to your face. Lightly scented aftershave is formulated to cool and soothe recently shaved skin; stronger cologne is not.

"Use cologne sparingly. The people around you should be just pleasantly aware of it, and it certainly shouldn't linger in the room after you've gone. Use even less on hot days—heat intensifies fragrance. Never store colognes in direct heat or sunlight, and throw away bottles that have been around longer than a year—a good cologne just doesn't smell the same after twelve months."

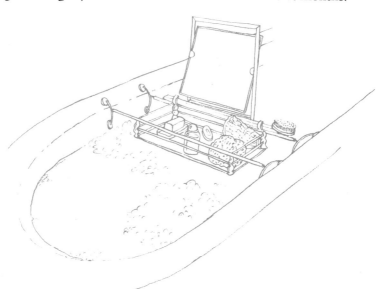

SATURDAY NIGHT BATHS

A daily shower is essential for keeping your skin free of dead cells that can decompose and cause body odor. It's a good solution—it wakes you up, braces the skin, and sends the dead cells down the drain. Constant showers, however, can dry and irritate your skin, so treat yourself to a good bath every week or so. A bath in oil-treated water can soothe your skin and help clear your mind. And frankly, it just feels good.

Before you run the bath water, you'll need bath granules or oils to add to the water. (A few drops of baby oil in the water or smoothed over the skin will also work.) If you want your bath to revive rather than relax you, toss some Epsom salts in the water.

As the tub fills, gather up the accessories you'll need—a pumice stone to slough off dead skin on heels and elbows; a loofah to scrub dead cells from your shoulders; a long-handled brush to scrub your back; a bar of hard-milled soap; and an orange stick to push back softened cuticles. If you don't have these things, check the men's cosmetic counter of any department store—leisurely baths aren't just for women anymore. Finish your bath by applying an astringent to tighten your pores. If your skin is dry, follow that with a body moisturizer.

FACIALS

To experience a good facial is to feel pampered. While some dermatologists feel that facials accomplish nothing that soap and water can't, others believe that they provide deep cleaning that helps prevent occasional break-outs. They're not for skin with severe problems, but there's no question that they will make healthy skin feel good and look better.

Facials vary from salon to salon, but you can expect at least some of the following during any facial:

A technician will examine your face under a magnifier to analyze the type of skin you have (normal, oily, or dry), where flareups may occur, and what problems you may have. After the analysis, you'll be taken to a private room and given a robe to wear. Once you're seated in a comfortable chair, a misting machine will moisten your skin and open the pores to prepare it for the facial massage. The massage, which may be done with creams, will relax your face and neck while cleaning the epidermis, toning the skin tissue, and stimulating circulation. If creams are used, they will be removed with cotton, and a soft brush may be used to gently scrub dirt from the skin's surface. The technician will remove blackheads and plugs from the pores.

When your face has been throughly cleaned in this way, the technician will apply a facial mask. You'll probably feel a cooling sensation at first, then warmth and a tightening of the skin. When the mask is removed, it will take dead skin cells with it, refreshing your complexion.

There are several different types of facial masks you can apply yourself at home. A *clay mask*, best suited for oily skin, has a mineral-clay base that hardens on your skin and absorbs dirt and oils. A *massaging mask*, good for normal and oily skin, has a plastic base and is applied to your face as a lotion or cream. After it's dry, you rub it off, taking dirt and dead cells with it. A *peel-off* mask, best suited to normal skin, is applied as a lotion or cream and then pulled off in one sheet when it's dry to refresh the skin. A *moisturizing mask*, for dry skin, has a jelly-like base that often includes protein. It cleans the skin and adds moisture.

No mask should be used too often. Regardless of skin type, they can be irritating and excessively drying. Once a week is enough to thoroughly cleanse your skin.

SKIN PROBLEMS

Very few people have perfect skin. Nearly everyone has an occasional pimple, blackhead, or clogged pores that need cleansing. It's not simply an adolescent problem—for many people, it's something that never completely goes away.

If you have serious skin problems—chronic or severe acne, allergic reactions, boils, or outbreaks of blotches or growths—don't try to treat them yourself. A dermatologist's expertise is necessary to diagnose and treat such problems properly. If, however, your skin simply isn't as clear and healthy looking as you'd like it to be, there's a lot you can do to make it look its best.

Contrary to myth, sweet or rich foods are not the leading cause of acne. The real culprits are your sebaceous glands, which normally protect your skin by supplying sebum, an oily substance composed of fats and waxes, to its surface. When present in proper amounts, sebum protects the skin from drying and eventually wrinkling. When the glands are overstimulated and produce too much sebum, however, your pores can become clogged and obstruct the normal flow of sebum to the skin's surface. The pressure of sebum building up behind the plug can cause a follicle wall to break, allowing sebum to spread into tissues below the skin. This creates an inflammation, or pimple.

It's unlikely that diet has much to do with acne, although some dermatologists believe that iodide (found in iodized salt, saltwater fish, and shellfish) can trigger outbreaks of inflammation in people prone to acne.

If you suffer from more than the occasional pimple, it's probably because your sebaceous glands are being overstimulated by one, or a combination of several, of the following reasons.

STRESS

You've probably noticed that your skin is most likely to break out when you have an important meeting or a significant business deal coming up. Even if your skin is not normally oily, your sebaceous glands will produce more oil when you're feeling nervous or pressured. Make sure you follow a scrupulous cleansing routine (see page 19) to discourage inflammation before it begins.

MEDICATION

A surprising variety of over-the-counter medications can trigger acne in some people. Be especially careful of those that contain bromides, cortisone (often found in poison-ivy treatments), and iodides (often found in cold medicines). If you're troubled by sudden and unusual bouts with acne, think about the medications you've been taking, and check the labels to see if they contain potentially acne-triggering substances. You may find that substituting another brand with different ingredients will eliminate your skin problems.

HEREDITY

It's a simple fact. If your parents had problems with acne, the chances are very high that you will too. You'll have to take exceptionally good care of your skin to avoid frequent inflammations.

No matter what condition your skin is in, it can be markedly improved by faithfully following a good cleansing and care routine.

TANNING

A good tan goes a long way toward making you look healthy and relaxed. Overdoing your sunning, however, is believed to cause certain types of skin cancer, and it can definitely prematurely wrinkle and age your skin. Obviously, moderation and preparation are the keys. When you tan, the sun's ultraviolet rays cause the color-producing protein in the outer layer of the skin, called melanin, to disperse. The amount of pigment in your skin determines whether you'll tan or burn. Fair-skinned people, without much pigment, are the most susceptible to sun-related problems. The American Medical Association recommends that fair-skinned people expose their unprotected skin to the sun for only fifteen minutes on the first day of the season, and an additional five minutes sun on the first day of the season, and an additional five minutes each day thereafter. The AMA guidelines for dark-skinned people are nearly as cautious—twenty minutes the first day, and an additional five minutes each subsequent day. You may want to adjust the guidelines to suit your situation: the sun over a midwestern pool is far less intense than at a tropical beach; you're more likely to burn quickly at high noon than at nine in the morning. Regardless of the circumstances, you'll be safest if you always use sun protection products and never allow your skin to be severely sunburned or excessively dark and leathery.

Find a good sun-protection product and calculate (before you take on the sun) how long you can safely stay. There are three types of products: *sun blocks* screen out the sun nearly completely; *sunscreens* block rays and permit a minimal amount of tanning, and *suntan lotions*, which come in different strengths, screen out some burning rays to allow you to tan freely. Whatever type you use, reapply it frequently as you sun, and always reapply it after you've been swimming.

Sun blocks, sun screens and tanning lotions are graded by number according to their Sun Protection Factor (SPF). For example, an SPF 6 means you should be able to stay in the sun without burning six times as long as you normally can without protection. Products with SPF ratings of 8 or more are by themselves drying to the skin. Always use a body and face moisturizer after use of these products and exposure to the sun and wind.

MANICURES

Well-groomed hands are certainly as important as well-shined shoes. And you can keep your hands looking their best with weekly at-home manicures. All you need is an emery board, an orange stick, a pumice stone, a hand lotion, and a nail buffer (all available at any department store cosmetic counter or drug store).

Begin by washing and drying your hands thoroughly. Nail clippers do a good job of shortening nails, as long as you follow the clippers with an emery board to smooth jagged edges that can cause hangnails and infections. (Weekly filing with an emery board should make clipping unnecessary.) Avoid metal nail files— they tend to wear and split nails.

To file, place the flat side of an emery board at the edge of your nail and draw it briskly to the center of the nail. Don't drag it back from the center to the edge—file in one direction only. When one side of the nail has been smoothed, begin at the opposite edge and file that side toward the center. Never file back and forth, which can cause splits and tears.

When you've filed all your nails to a smooth, rounded edge, soak your fingertips in a bowl filled with soapy water (a capful of dishwashing liquid will do fine) for five minutes. This cleanses the

nails and softens the cuticles. If your nails are stained, scrub them lightly under the water with a nail brush.

Set the bowl of water aside and use an orange stick to gently push back the cuticles growing over the base of the nail. Never cut cuticles—they're there to protect the skin surrounding the nails from tearing and becoming infected.

Next, take the pumice stone and rub it lightly around each of your nails to sand away dead skin. Submerge your hands in the bowl of soapy water for a minute or two to remove traces of pumice and dead skin, then rinse them under cool running water.

Dry them well and apply the hand lotion, making sure to rub it into the cuticles and the skin surrounding the nails.

When the lotion has been completely absorbed, "polish" your nails with the buffer using a brisk, light back-and-forth motion. Don't overdo it—you want your nails to gleam slightly, not to shine.

TEETH

Your teeth are one of the first things that people notice about you, so proper dental care is essential to an attractive appearance. Even more important, dental care is essential to your general health. Having a minimal number of cavities doesn't necessarily mean your mouth is healthy. (Most people begin getting fewer cavities once they reach their twenties.) The threat of periodontitis, the gum disease that is the major cause of adult tooth loss, is constant and can only be controlled through a diligent program of tooth and gum care. Periodontitis begins with plaque, a sticky, colorless layer of bacteria that is constantly forming on the enamel of your teeth. In its early stages, plaque is 80 percent water, but it quickly hardens into a deposit called tartar. This tartar painlessly dissolves the calcium of your teeth and irritates the gums. Eventually, the teeth grow loose in the gums and fall out. Only a professional cleaning by your dentist can remove hardened tartar from teeth. Once the tartar is removed, your goal is to keep it from forming again. Brushing your teeth carefully twice a day is a good start, but it's not enough.

A TOOTH CARE ROUTINE

In addition to a toothbrush, get in the habit of using toothpicks and dental floss. In the morning, brush as you always have. Each night, before you brush your teeth, wrap each end of an eighteen-inch length of dental floss around the middle finger of each hand, leaving a three- or four-inch length in between. Holding the floss taut, work it gently up and down between each tooth. Next, curve it and floss around each tooth to scrape plaque from its surface. Finally, use the rounded end of a toothpick to gently scrape the area between gum and tooth. When you've finished, brush all the loosened matter away with your toothbrush. Brushing properly takes at least two minutes, brushing down on the upper teeth, up on the lower teeth, and back and forth over the surface of the molars.

CORRECTING PROBLEMS

Crooked, chipped, protruding, or missing teeth are all correctible problems. Slightly irregular teeth are nothing to worry about—nearly everyone has some slight imperfections—but if you'd prefer to improve your smile, there are many ways to do it.

Caps: Teeth that are broken, chipped, or badly decayed can be capped. (In the case of decayed teeth, the decayed areas will have to be removed before they can be capped.) The tooth to be capped is ground down and fitted with a gold crown topped with a porcelain cap that's tinted to match the color of your natural teeth. Caps are permanent and will not decay.

False Teeth: If you're missing a tooth, the teeth on either side of the space can be used as anchors for a bridge that holds a replacement tooth.

Braces: They're not just for kids anymore. Some types, made of thin wires encased in clear plastic, are nearly invisible. If your teeth protrude because your mouth is crowded, some teeth may have to be extracted before the braces are put on.

PLASTIC SURGERY

If something about your appearance seriously disturbs you, consider having it surgically corrected. If your ears stick out, your tattoo or acne scars embarrass you, your nose is too big, or your face has developed jowls or bags under the eyes, a good plastic surgeon can help. This is not a decision to be made lightly. Any surgery performed under anesthetic can be hazardous, and it'll be a while before the bruises to go away. Don't rush—cosmetic surgery isn't an emergency procedure, so take your time looking for a good doctor. Ask your friends for recommendations and consult with several before going ahead with surgery.

TO SUM UP...

- Daily showers are fine for keeping your skin clean and free of dead cells, but they can be drying. A bath once a week is the perfect opportunity to moisturize your skin and relax at the same time.

- When wearing a fragrance, apply it sparingly. People around you should be pleasantly aware of the fragrance, not overpowered by it.

- A tan looks terrific, but overexposure to the sun has been linked to certain types of skin cancer and will prematurely weather and age your skin. *Always* protect your skin with products that contain a sun protection factor, and limit the amount of time you spend in the sun.

- After shaving, follow up with an application of astringent aftershave to close pores and heal the tiny nicks that shaving creates.

HAIR CARE

Good hair care is very much like good skin care—cleanliness is the key. And like healthy skin, healthy hair begins on the inside. A proper diet and exercise regime will tone your hair as well as the rest of your body. But even shiny, healthy hair will benefit from a little extra care. To many men, hair care and styling is a mystery—one that they're more comfortable leaving to women. But any man can have better looking hair without going to a lot of trouble.

It's important to understand that your hair has something of a will of its own. It may be dry or oily, frizzy or limp, cooperative or stubborn, but once you're aware of its quirks you'll be able to choose and easily maintain a flattering style.

Don't subscribe to hair myths. Frequent shampooing will do no harm—unless you're using a shampoo that's too harsh for your hair type, and/or failing to rinse your hair properly. According to Frank Barbuscio of Shulton Inc., "Hair is very similar to skin. The protein in hair and the protein in skin are very similar. You wash your face several times a day and as long as you don't use a harsh, drying soap, it won't harm your skin. There's no reason why you can't wash your hair at least once a day. You won't hurt your hair. You can't cause baldness by washing and blow-drying your hair."

HAIR TYPES

Hair type depends on the production of sebum, a natural oily secretion from the sebaceous glands in the scalp. It coats the hair shaft and acts as a kind of a natural trap for grease, grime, dust, and dirt. Your hair type (oily, normal, or dry) is determined by the amount of sebum your scalp produces. Recognizing your hair type is easy. If your hair needs to be washed every day or two to look fluffy and shiny, it's oily. If your hair is dull or brittle-looking several days after a shampoo, it's dry. If your hair doesn't ever seem to get especially greasy or brittle, and two shampoos a week (under ordinary circumstances) keep it looking good, it's normal.

SHAMPOOING

Choose a shampoo formulated for your hair type. All shampoos should remove surface dust and dirt and leave your hair soft and manageable. Select a shampoo that contains a conditioning ingredient—the label will tell you if it does or not—which eliminates the need for a frequent separate conditioning step. Experiment with a few brands to determine which ones are best for your hair. (You'll have to use each product you sample for at least a week or two to judge its effectiveness.)

Whatever shampoo you choose, remember that it should be mild. Since you'll probably be shampooing frequently to keep your hair in top condition, there's no reason to use a product full of harsh soaps and detergents. Under normal circumstances, your hair simply isn't dirty enough to need them. (You should, of course, always shampoo after strenuous exercise or after exposing your hair to salt or chlorinated water.) Any shampoo will be more effective if you use it properly:

- Using your fingertips, make sure you massage the shampoo into every inch of your scalp.

- Don't overshampoo. The instructions on most bottles

"I think that men are taking better care of their hair than they used to. The average man I see today has healthier, better-looking hair than the average man did five or six years ago."
—TEDDY DONIFRIO, barber

specify lathering your hair twice, but unless your hair is unusually greasy or grimy, you don't need to. One thorough washing will be enough.

- Shampoo under the shower rather than in a bath. The constant flow of spray is stimulating to the scalp and ideal for rinsing thoroughly.

- Rinsing is critical to washing your hair well. Even after you're sure you've gotten all the suds out, rinse an extra thirty seconds or so. In all, you should rinse your hair for between one and two full minutes. Flakes of dried shampoo trapped in hair are often mistaken for dandruff. (You can make your hair shine by finishing the rinse with a few seconds of icy cold water.)

CONDITIONING

A separate conditioning step after you shampoo can revitalize your hair, restoring the protein that shampooing strips away and giving hair a healthy sheen, as long as you don't overdo it. Men's shorter hair can quickly become limp and lifeless from constant conditioning.

MOUSSE

Mousse is an excellent styling tool that combines the benefits of hair spray and conditioner. It allows you to style your hair and then maintain that style by reducing the static that results from combing, thus eliminating "flyaway" hair.

Like conditioners, mousse can be overused and build up on your hair. Ideally you should shampoo between applications of mousse —never use mousse more than twice between shampoos.

It's important to find the amount that works best for the amount of hair you have. A golf ball sized puff of mousse is average; you can increase or decrease that amount according to your hair's thickness. Towel dry your hair, then rub the mousse between your palms and work it into your damp hair evenly and thoroughly, coating the hair shafts as completely as you can. When you've finished massaging in the mousse, style and blow dry your hair as you would normally.

STYLING WITH A BLOW DRYER

Blow dryer styling is really very simple. Watch the stylist style your hair first, and ask him to give you a step-by-step explanation of what he's doing so you can get the same results at home. Remember, though, that blow dryers should be used as styling tools, not to dry hair that's soaking wet. Always towel-dry your hair gently until it's just damp, then turn on the dryer to style your hair.

These simple tips from barber Teddy Donifrio will help you get the most from your blow dryer:

- If your dryer doesn't have a special brush attachment, get a round styling brush and a wide-tooth comb to use with the dryer.

- To style, brush your hair into the contours you want, sweeping the dryer along immediately behind the brush.

- When your hair is dry and styled, brush it straight back, then comb it into place. The style should look completely natural.

BRUSHES AND COMBS

A natural bristle brush is best for your hair and scalp, but they're expensive—a good brush, such as those made by Kent of London, can cost anywhere between $50 and $100. "Most of the brushes have nylon or plastic bristles nowadays," says Donifrio. "You can use them, but you have to be careful not to dig them into the scalp because their synthetic bristles can easily scratch the skin. The advantage of natural bristles is that you can use the brush to massage the scalp and there won't be any scratching."

Plastic combs can also dig into the scalp, causing scratches and possibly infection. Donifrio recommends that you use a hard rubber comb, such as those made by Ace, which won't scratch or tear skin.

"If you let your hair grow for more than four weeks it gets completely out of shape, so when you do have it cut, it looks radically different from the way it did the day before. If you keep it neat by having it trimmed every three to four weeks, you'll never look like a farmer who just came to town to get a haircut."
—TEDDY DONIFRIO, *barber*

BEARDS AND MOUSTACHES

Growing a beard or moustache takes patience. They need about four weeks to shape up, so you'll have to endure a month or so of looking like you've forgotten to shave. But it can be worth it. A beard and/or moustache can hide facial scars, add character, and just generally improve your appearance.

Proportion is the key. You don't want to overwhelm a thin face with a bushy beard and moustache, and you can't balance your bald head with a long beard. If you're unsure about what look is best for you, consult a hair stylist for advice.

Once you've grown a beard or moustache, it requires care. Facial hair can trap perspiration, so shampoo it whenever you shampoo your hair. And grooming is essential—comb and brush your beard and moustache frequently, and trim them every few days.

COPING WITH GREY

Although it is considerably more acceptable for a man to dye his hair than it was a dozen years ago, it's still not a decision to be made in haste. "I'm rather shocked at all the men who are now dyeing their hair," says Geoffrey Beene. "I was on the Concorde recently, and there wasn't a man with a crooked nose or grey hair. All these men had jet-black hair, which seemed silly, since they'd never had jet-black hair before in their lives."

If you are bothered by the presence of prematurely grey hair (which many people find attractive and distinguished) and believe that dyeing your hair will improve your appearance, proceed with caution. Ideally, a stylist whom you trust should dye it for you to assure the best possible results. He'll use the same products you can use at home, but his skill and experience will enable him to attain the color that's best for you.

If you do it yourself, any one of the reputable products that are normally advertised for women will work just as well for you. They come in dozens of shades; be careful to choose one that approximates your natural hair color. (Because the color pictured on the box won't exactly match the dye's actual shade, it's a good idea to snip a bit of hair from the back of your head and sample-color it before you dye all your hair.) Follow the directions on the package closely.

HAIR LOSS

Thinning hair and baldness can be caused by a variety of factors—improper diet, excessive stress, medications, illness—but the vast majority of hair loss is the result of a process called "male-pattern baldness," a somewhat ill-understood phenomenon related to the production of testosterone. (Women are rarely subject to baldness simply because they do not produce testosterone.) Your chances of falling prey to male-pattern baldness are largely based on heredity; if your father or grandfather suffered from it, chances are you will too. If you haven't lost a fairly significant amount of hair by your thirtieth birthday, you'll probably never suffer from male-pattern baldness.

Male-pattern baldness usually follows a depressingly predictable course. First, the hairline recedes. Next, the hair at the crown thins. These two hairless areas work toward each other, leaving the top of the head bald. (Most men retain a fairly abundant fringe of hair around the sides and back of the head.)

One of the best ways to deal with baldness is to accept it. Resist the temptation to let the hair you do have grow and use it to conceal the bald spots. It doesn't work. Baldness can be attractive; handling it badly never is.

"It's a highly personal decision," says Maurice Mann, president of Hair Again, Ltd., a company that offers many options to men seeking to replace lost hair. "There is no right answer. You can do just as well in life without having hair on your head as you can with it. It's an individual choice, analogous to a decision to invest in contact lenses, cap your teeth, or have a face lift.

"I think anyone interested in hair replacement has to be very careful about where he goes, the method he chooses, and why he chooses it. Because the industry in general is not regulated by any federal, state, or city agency, there are a lot of compromising entrepreneurs. The consumer has to be very careful."

"There's no time for a man to recover his hair that grows bald by nature."
—WILLIAM SHAKESPEARE

If you can't accept the thought of life without a full head of hair, you do have some options. None of them is without drawbacks, so consider each carefully to decide which is best for you.

37

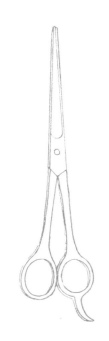

NON-SURGICAL ALTERNATIVES

Minoxidil, a drug that experts believe may eventually be the perfect solution to baldness, is still in the experimental stages. Originally developed as a treatment for high blood pressure, minoxidil, when applied topically, stimulates dormant hair follicles beneath the skin to grow hair. In its present state, minoxidil must be applied to the scalp every day to keep the follicles stimulated. Currently being tested by Upjohn, it is several years away from being generally available.

A *toupee* is a hairpiece built up from a base that's shaped like the bald spot to be concealed and attached to the scalp with double-sided tape. Available in synthetic or human hair, toupees have a poor reputation, mainly because there are so many bad ones around.

The toupee is the oldest form of hair replacement available. As a rule, if the hairpiece is made properly, you can't detect it. It's the bad ones that everybody is able to pick out. Most men in their twenties and thirties, however, are not psychologically comfortable with a hairpiece because the sterotype says that only a suburban middle-aged man with three kids will be wearing one. But a toupee, if properly made, can be a very acceptable alternative.

If you decide a toupee is the solution to your hair problems, it's worth the expense of having a good one custom-made for you. Actually, you'll need to have two, since you'll need a spare when one is being cleaned. The major drawback of a toupee is that you simply can't wear it all the time—you'll have to remove it to sleep, swim, and shower, and there's always the possibility it may slip or change position during vigorous physical activity. However, if you accept a toupee as a cosmetic improvement—not an attempt to fool the entire world into thinking that's all your hair—it may be right for you. A good toupee will cost between $500 and $1,000.

Hairweaving is comparable to blending a toupee in with your hair semipermanently. "Hairweaving is a very tricky area," says Mann, "in the sense that it is marketed by different companies throughout the country as anything but hairweaving. There are a lot of different trade names for it—Permalock, Strand-by-Strand, One Hair At A Time, Fusion Method, Durmalock—but in the final analysis, it's all very much the same. "The only difference between methods is whether or not the hairweave technique in question uses a foundation."

When a foundation is used, a nylon lattice is placed over the bald spot, and surrounding hairs are braided and woven around the edges of the lattice to hold it firmly in place. Strands of your own hair, supplemented by synthetic and/or human hair, are woven into the lattice base until it is concealed by hair. Once completed, the hairweave is "permanent" in that you can swim, shower, and sleep in it. The problem with foundations is that your own natural hair, after a few showers, can get caught underneath the foundation, where it tends to mat and pull.

In all types of hairweaving, your own hair will continue to grow on the sides and in the back. As it grows, the replacement hair becomes loose. You'll need to return to the hairweaver approximately every six weeks, depending on how fast your hair grows. Some men only need to have it tightened every two months, but that's the maximum amount of time it can possibly last. After that, it starts to get loose and it doesn't look good. There are companies that will tell you can wait three months or more between maintenance visits, but that's simply not true. A hairweave can cost between $600 and $1200; the average maintenance visit lasts a few hours and costs $50.

SURGICAL ALTERNATIVES
Skin grafting is a method of anchoring a hairpiece by grafting a thin strip of skin, usually taken from the groin, to the scalp to create a tunnel into which hairpiece clips can be inserted. Although a hairpiece anchored by this method is far less likely to accidentally

slip out of position than a conventional toupee, it should still be removed for sleeping and vigorous activity because the clips can irritate or even tear through the skin grafts. This technique costs several hundred dollars.

Hair transplants, which can be time-consuming and painful, are very effective for small bald patches that are not the result of an ongoing pattern of baldness. Small sections of hair, skin, follicles, and fat, called "plugs," are taken from the back and sides of the head and surgically implanted into the bald areas. After a few months of adjustment, the plugs begin—and continue—to produce hair.

Most men who choose hair transplants are under the illusion that they're going to stop their continuing hair loss in areas where the hair is thinned but not yet gone. This is a fantasy. A transplant is only redistributing hair, not adding more to your head. You'll wind up with a very thin combing of hair over the bald area, which is fine as long as you don't expect anything more.

"I think transplants work best in specific, isolated circumstances," says Mann. "If someone has a small bald spot, maybe the size of a half dollar, on the crown or hairline area, a transplant can be the perfect solution. But they don't work for someone who's trying to thicken an entire head of hair."

The problem with transplants is a simple matter of mathematics. The average head has approximately 100,000 individual hairs. The maximum number of grafts that any one person can undergo is 350 to 500. Each plug contains fifteen hairs. Even with optimum conditions and 500 plugs, that's 7,500 hairs, or 7.5 percent of a full head of hair.

If you think a transplant would be right for you, remember that it can be a time-consuming process. Some companies will put in as many as one hundred plugs per session, but most try to minimize trauma to the scalp by doing fifty or sixty per session. Sessions are scheduled six to eight weeks apart, and until the process is completed you may suffer a swollen scalp and some discomfort. Once the plugs are in, the area surrounding them will form scabs. The scabs eventually fall off, and the hair in the transplanted plugs falls out from the trauma of being moved. In a few months, the plugs begin producing hair. In spite of their inconvenience, the success rate of transplants is virtually 100 percent, although some of the plugs may be rejected and new ones have to be inserted in their place. The average transplant usually costs between $500 and $1,000.

If you're planning a transplant, ask at least two doctors or reputable hair-replacement companies (the good companies will be affiliated with a qualified dermatologist) for their opinions about your case.

The *cosmetic surgery suture process* differs from transplants in that it doesn't simply transfer existing hair. Instead, surgical sutures are put into the fatty surface of the scalp, a process that takes about thirty minutes. The sutures, made of a plastic fiber, act as a foundation. Strips of combined natural and synthetic hair, called wefts, are attached directly to the exposed part of the suture. The man's natural hair continues to grow around and through the sutures. When completed, there are tiers of hair, almost like shingles on a roof.

"We've found that a combination of synthetic and natural hair, in about an 80:20 ratio, works best," notes Mann. "The synthetic hair is less likely to mat when wet than human hair is. The synthetic hair gets wet, looks wet, and acts wet, but it doesn't absorb water. Human hair acts like a sponge, and can feel uncomfortably heavy on the head when it's wet. Human hair is dead tissue; it's going to go straight and stay limp after a few washings. The blend of natural and synthetic hair gives a man a sense of having human hair with all the practicality of the synthetic. The texture isn't identical to that of human hair, but it's reasonably close."

Since the sutures don't cut or lacerate the skin, there's no real pain involved. The sutures are placed while the man is under local anesthetic, the hair is attached, and then he goes home. There's no need for the scalp to heal—there are only small entry and exit points for the stitches. He may have a slight headache when the anesthetic wears off, but in a day or so he's fine.

As long as the sutures are kept clean and the man is fairly gentle with them—as a contact-lens wearer would be when he rubbed his eyes—he shouldn't have any more problems. He can swim, shower, shampoo, and exercise with no problems. He'll have to return once every two years to have the wefts of hair changed and to have the sutures checked. A suture can be replaced very easily if it's migrated slightly, which sometimes happens. And, unlike transplants, if a man decides he doesn't want to have hair, the sutures can be removed without scarring. The cosmetic surgery suture process costs between $1,500 and $2,500. The replacement process costs approximately $1,000.

Synthetic hair fiber implants have recently been banned by the Food and Drug Administration because they nearly always cause scalp infection, swelling, and scarring. If you find a company that offers this method, don't even consider doing business with them.

THE PSYCHOLOGY OF HAIR REPLACEMENT

A realistic attitude is essential when considering any hair-replacement technique. Having hair again is not going to change your life. "We occasionally get an ordinary-looking man who comes in and shows us a photograph of the model he'd like to resemble," Mann says. "I've taught our stylists to be very direct. They'll say to him, 'You will *never* look like this guy. Now let's see how we can make you look better.' There's no point in building up false hope. This is about hair replacement, not psychiatry."

No matter which hair-replacement method you choose, don't keep it a secret. The experience of having hair again, while undeniably pleasant, can also be somewhat traumatic. That trauma isn't helped any by the shocked stares you may get from unwarned friends and family when you suddenly appear with hair. You'll make the transition much easier on yourself if you let those close to you know what you're doing.

TO SUM UP...

- Blow dryers should be used for styling, not for drying drenched hair. Towel-dry gently but thoroughly first.

- Natural bristle brushes and hard rubber combs are the best choice for your hair and scalp.

- Beards and moustaches can improve your appearance, as long as they're in proportion to your face and body.

- Cleanliness and conditioning are the keys to keeping hair looking its best.

- Have your hair trimmed every three to four weeks.

- A good hair style is the result of a collaboration between you and a stylist. You have to know what you want and talk to the stylist about it before he begins cutting.

- If you choose to dye your hair, do it carefully. Avoid those products that eliminate grey gradually, and always perform a skin sensitivity test before applying the dye.

- If your hair is especially limp or frizzy, you can have a permanent to curl or straighten it.

- There are a variety of methods for dealing with hair loss, and the one you choose depends on your lifestyle, personal needs, and the type of hair loss you have. No hair-replacement technique can drastically alter your life or looks.

THE TRIM LOOK

The dogma is simple and virtually everyone accepts it—a man should eat a balanced, healthy diet, and exercise with some consistency. What's there to argue about? But getting on with such a simple plan is far from simple. For most of us it means developing new habits and replacing bad habits with good ones. At stake is how much control over your life you will have while you're here—how much trouble will you have with your health? How vital will you be? What will be the quality of your life? And if you're looking for quality, then you have to do certain things. The first step in this lifelong path is to get some information and then apply it. Chief among those certain things is to pay closer attention to diet and to develop a pattern of regular exercise.

A study conducted by the Washington D.C.-based Brookings Institute drew the conclusion that of the many personal elements necessary for successful business leadership, the leading factor is physical condition and endurance. The other factors—intelligence, ability to lead, to compromise, to synthesize, and attention to detail, don't matter if you're not healthy enough to demonstrate them.

And if that isn't reason enough to pay attention to your body, consider this. You can confirm it easily. Most men, when they meet another man for the first time, or when they see an acquaintance after a relatively lengthy interval, look or at least glance at the other man's stomach. And they compare it with their own. Why would you give away that edge?

A HEALTHY DIET

Eating to achieve and maintain maximum health isn't complicated. Assuming you don't have any specific health problems, you need to consume dairy products, vegetables, fruits, breads, cereals, and a limited amount of meat to stay healthy. Your body requires protein, fat, and carbohydrates to furnish heat and energy.

The keys to a healthy diet are moderation and variety. Fad diets that depend on consuming only one type of food aren't healthy, and even if they were you probably wouldn't stick with them because they quickly become boring. A varied diet is more enjoyable and ensures that your body will be receiving the complete range of essential vitamins and nutrients.

Diet books and diet plans abound, but not every diet is suited to every person. And some really aren't suited to anybody. Losing weight safely—and keeping it off—is a slow process. It's essential that you don't sacrifice the nutrients your body needs while you're trying to cut down on calories.

Low-calorie diets, probably the most sensible of all diet plans, have a very simple premise: you must consume fewer calories than your body burns. This kind of diet requires only willpower and common sense—you must choose the quantities and types of food that you eat carefully, always keeping the calorie total below a certain maximum level. You eat all foods in moderation, and lose up to three pounds a week.

Low-carboyhydrate diets are trickier to manage. They require that you keep your consumption of carbohydrates (found in sugar, starches, and breads) between 50 and 60 grams per day. This balance can be difficult to maintain—a ceiling of 60 grams of carbohydrate is very low for the average American's diet, and if you get overzealous and consume fewer than 50 grams per day you'll feel fatigued. You'll need to carry a carbohydrate-gram counter with you at all times. This diet is based on the premise that if your carbohydrate intake is very low, your body reacts by burning its fat reserves. You can eat anything you like as long as you stay within your carbohydrate limit, and you'll lose about two pounds a week.

High-protein diets usually consist of lean meat, a limited amount of dairy products, practically no carbohydrates, and a lot of liquid. This diet forces your body to break down its fatty tissue to supply energy. You'll lose weight fairly rapidly on this sort of diet—about five pounds a week—but you won't be doing your body any good. You'll eat the same few foods day after day (the sheer dullness of it all may cause you to eat less), and these foods do not supply your body with the vitamins and minerals it needs. You'll need to take supplements. Fatty acid residues produced by this diet can be irritating to the kidneys and liver and must be flushed out with great quantities of water. Such diets can be dangerous for people with a history of kidney or liver problems, and they cause bad breath in everyone. They're also extremely boring.

GUIDELINES FOR A HEALTHIER DIET

EAT LIGHT

Increase the amount of fresh fish, chicken, turkey, and veal in your diet, while decreasing your intake of red meat and shellfish (ground turkey substitutes nicely for ground beef in most recipes). These revisions will help you reduce your consumption of cholesterol, which most men should cut by about half. When present in excessive amounts, cholesterol is linked to heart disease, but it is an essential element. It is a part of the structure of nearly all body tissues, particularly those in the brain and nervous system, and it also aids in the production of bile, which allows the digestive tract to absorb the fat-soluable vitamins A, D, E, and K.

Try poaching and broiling foods rather than frying them or dressing them with heavy sauces. You can also reduce your cholesterol intake painlessly by using only egg whites instead of whole eggs, cutting out whole-milk dairy products and replacing them with the skim or low-fat varieties, and reducing the amount of fat you normally use to sauté foods.

Avoid saturated fats, which can leave fatty deposits on the walls of arteries and restrict blood flow. Saturated fats are found in milk, cream, eggs, butter, lard, hydrogenated fats, cheese, and shellfish. Unsaturated fats include oils made from corn, peanuts, olives, safflowers, sunflowers, wheat germ, soy beans, and margarine made without hydrogenated fat.

Never stuff yourself with any foods, no matter how healthy they may be. Your digestive tract has to struggle to break down excessive amounts of food so your body uses the food less efficiently. You're far less likely to overeat if you learn to eat slowly. It takes some time for your stomach to register the fact that it's full, so give it a chance.

Skip the extras. Pass up the bread and butter before dinner, trim the fat from meat, remove the skin from poultry, and don't use gravy or rich sauces.

AVOID SALT AND SUGAR

Eating salt- or sugar-laden foods is a habit you'd do well to break. The taste for salt and sugar is an acquired one, and it can be overcome.

The average diet supplies six times more salt than your body requires, and too much salt is believed to contribute to high blood pressure, heart disease, and kidney failure. Instead of salting your food, try substituting flavorful herbs and spices in cooking, or seasoning with pepper or onions. Avoid foods that contain large amounts of salt, such as bacon, ham, frankfurters, and salted nuts.

Sugar in any form, including raw sugar and honey, is high in calories and low in nutrients. (In fact, studies show that honey rots teeth faster and contains more calories than the same quantity of white sugar.) About 20 percent of the average man's total calorie consumption is composed of sugar; experts recommend that this be reduced by at least half. Cutting sugar out of your coffee and eliminating the occasional candy bar isn't enough—you may very well be consuming vast amounts of "hidden" sugar. According to a consumer group, the Center for Science in the Public Interest, twelve ounces of Pepsi-Cola contains ten teaspoons of sugar, ten jellybeans contain nearly seven teaspoons of sugar, a five-ounce slice of pecan pie contains twelve teaspoons of sugar, and one cup of Dannon yogurt with fruit contains nearly eight teaspoons of sugar. To determine the true amount of sugar in any food, check its label for the words sucrose, dextrose, corn syrup, honey, brown sugar, raw sugar, molasses, fructose, and high-fructose corn sugar. Since ingredients present in the greatest amount are given first, you may very well find that several of these sugars are scattered throughout the list of ingredients.

While sugar does supply the body with needed glucose, you can also obtain glucose from most fruits and starches.

LOOK BEYOND NATURAL

A completely natural food has had no artificial chemicals, colors, emulsifiers, flavor enhancers, or other ingredients added to it during processing or packaging. Foods that fit this description are unquestionably more healthful than foods laden with additives and synthetics that your body isn't designed to digest or utilize.

It would be nice if you could improve your health and appearance by eating only those foods labeled "natural," but it isn't that easy. There is no widely accepted definition for the word "natural." Instead, its meaning varies from manufacturer to manufacturer and from consumer to consumer. Some "natural" foods are made with no artificial preservatives or flavorings but contain large amounts of sodium—sometimes far more than is found in "non-natural" versions of the same product. Other natural foods contain no white sugar but do contain large amounts of honey and other nonrefined sweeteners that are no more beneficial to health than white sugar.

In fact, very few genuinely pure, untouched foods exist. (Any commercially available item has been processed in some fashion—

at the very least, it has been cleaned and packaged.) And there's really nothing wrong with that. Many foods have substances added to them to improve their color, flavor, nutritional properties, or shelf life, and there's nothing wrong with that either—as long as the additives used are substances that occur in nature or that your body can utilize.

READ THE LABEL

Check a product's label for its list of ingredients. The ingredient present in the largest amount will be listed first, followed by the other ingredients in descending weight order. All additives used in a product, except flavors and colors, must also be listed by name. Colors and flavors must be mentioned, but need not be specified. The list of ingredients can simply say "artificial color," "artificial flavor," or "natural flavor." Although you probably can't avoid additives entirely, do avoid those foods with labels that feature long lists of chemicals and preservatives. Chances are the additive-laden foods contain few, if any, elements that your body needs.

NUTRITIONISTS

If you're genuinely puzzled about devising a healthy eating plan for yourself, or if you feel that your diet has been so inadequate you need some help to turn it around, you may want to consult a registered dietitian who has been certified by the American Dietetic Association. Be wary of people who bill themselves simply as "nutritionists." While many of these people offer sound and safe advice, many others are selling a blend of fact and myth. There are no legal standards for nutritionists. While some self-styled nutritionists have studied at unaccredited schools, others may simply have sent $50 to the American Association of Nutrition and Dietary Consultants and received a diploma in return.

Even the word "doctor" in front of his name does not necessarily indicate that a nutritionist is a certified M.D. In fact, Dr. Robert Haas, the best-selling author of *Eat To Win*, is not a medical doctor. He holds a master's degree in nutrition from Florida State University and a Ph.D. in nutrition from a nonaccredited correspondence school, Columbia Pacific University, based in San Rafael, California.

Avoid nutritionists who claim that hair analysis—in which a small amount of hair is clipped from your head and "analyzed" to determine your body's level of vitamins and minerals—can reveal dietary deficiencies. Hair never contains any vitamins, and it picks up an array of minerals, chemicals, and other substances from the environment. And, since hair consists of dead tissue that grew out of the scalp weeks or even months before it's clipped, it can only reflect past—not current—mineral levels. Blood and urine analyses are far more reliable methods of detecting the body's deficiencies.

The best way to find a registered dietitian is to ask your physician to recommend one. If he can't, the American Dietetic Association in Chicago can give you a list of registered dieticians in your area. Their telphone number is (312) 280-5000.

THE IMPORTANCE OF EXERCISE

A healthy diet will help you keep your weight down and maintain good general health, but without an accompanying exercise program your body will never be as well-toned or work as efficiently as it can. And following an effective exercise regime will allow you consume more calories than you can if you're sedentary.

The following chart, devised by Ronald Dunton and used in the Whitney Program, an adaptation training system that concentrates on improving health through behavior modification, illustrates the calories burned in one hour of different types of exercise. Note that your weight affects the number of calories your body burns.

CALORIE BURN RATE

WEIGHT	125	135	145	150	160	170	180	190	200	210	220	230	240
						CALORIES							
Walking, slowly (2 mph)[1]	175	185	200	210	220	235	240	260	275	300	310	320	335
Walking, fast (4.5 mph)[2]	330	350	375	400	420	445	470	490	520	560	585	610	630
Bicycling, slowly (5.5 mph)	250	265	285	300	320	335	350	370	395	425	440	460	480
Bicycling, vigorously (15 mph)	535	575	610	650	685	725	760	800	840	910	950	990	1025
Rowing, vigorously	685	730	780	825	875	925	970	1020	1070	1160	1210	1260	1310
Jogging, slowly (5.5 mph)[3]	535	575	610	650	685	725	760	800	840	910	950	990	1025
Jogging, moderately (7 mph)[4]	700	745	795	845	895	940	990	1040	1095	1190	1240	1285	1335

BEGINNING AN EXERCISE PROGRAM

Just as a sensibly healthy diet can be incorporated into your lifestyle with a minimum of disruption, an exercise routine can easily be made part of your everyday activities. Once exercise becomes a habit, it will require surpisingly little of your attention.

PATIENCE

If you've never followed a regular diet and exercise routine before, your eagerness to see the results of your new program may tempt

CALORIE BURN RATE

WEIGHT	125	135	145	150	160	170	180	190	200	210	220	230	240
							CALORIES						
Running, (9 mph)[5]	775	830	885	940	990	1050	1190	1160	1220	1320	1375	1430	1485
Country, skiing moderately	585	625	665	700	750	790	830	870	920	995	1035	1075	1120
Swimming, leisurely	240	250	275	290	300	320	340	350	380	405	425	440	460
Swimming, vigorously	437	465	500	525	555	590	620	650	685	740	770	805	835
Handball, continuous	485	520	560	590	625	660	690	725	765	830	865	900	935
Soccer	445	475	510	540	570	600	630	665	700	760	790	805	855
Tennis, vigorous singles	485	520	560	590	625	660	690	725	765	830	865	900	935
Volleyball, vigorous	485	520	560	590	625	660	690	725	765	830	865	900	935

[1] *this pace is very leisurely: 1 mile in 30 minutes*
[2] *this pace is very brisk: 1 mile in 13.3 minutes*
[3] *a leisurely jog: 1 mile in 10.9 minutes*
[4] *a typical jog: 1 mile in 8.5 minutes*
[5] *definitely a run: 1 mile in 6 minutes, 40 seconds*

you to do too much too soon. Resist the temptation. You won't really gain anything but sore muscles. And, even worse, the aches and pains you'll develop, combined with the fact that you won't see results overnight, may discourage you. A successful diet and exercise program is one that sets small daily and weekly goals—a two-pound per week weight loss rather than a twenty-pound loss. You'll be more aware of your successes if you divide the large goal into small ones.

DOCTOR'S ORDERS

Speak with your doctor before making any drastic changes in your diet or exercise habits. If you are healthy and simply plan to increase your level of activity, follow these medical guidelines suggested by aerobics expert Dr. Kenneth Cooper:

- If you're under thirty and have had, and passed, a physical exam within the past year, you can start exercising.

- If you're between thirty and thirty-nine, you should have a physical within three months of beginning your exercise program. It should include an electrocardiogram taken while you're at rest.

- If you're between forty and fifty-nine, you should have a physical within three months of beginning your exercise program, and an electrocardiogram should be taken while you're exercising.

- If you're over fifty-nine, you should have a physical immediately before you begin your exercise program. It should include an electrocardiogram taken while you're exercising.

TYPES OF EXERCISE

Overall fitness has three separate aspects—flexibility, strength, and endurance—and each is developed and maintained by a different kind of exercise.

Aerobic exercises build endurance by putting a heavy and constant demand on the heart and lungs. Typical aerobic exercises include walking, running, bicycling, swimming, jumping rope, tennis, and squash. In addition to toning the cardiovascular system, these exercises also improve your coordination and general muscle tone.

Anaerobic exercises, which include calisthenics, weight training, and Nautilus machine work-outs, aid in the development of flexibility, coordination, and strength while producing a limited amount of aerobic benefits. Anaerobics include isometric exercises, which build strength by inducing hard contractions within a muscle, or set of muscles, for a few seconds at a time. Typical isometric manuevers include pushing against an immovable object, such as a wall, or using opposing forces, such as pressing one palm against the other. If temporary health problems prevent you from carrying out more strenuous aerobic exercises, you can usually maintain your exercise routine by carrying out a modified series of anaerobic exercises to keep your body in condition until you're well enough to resume all your activities.

PUTTING IT TOGETHER

No single form of exercise provides everything that the human body is known to need in order to be optimally healthy and keep down the incidence of unnecessary illness. A number of recent reports issued by the American Medical Association have confirmed that an individual needs a combination of flexibility inducing exercises, aerobic exercise, some primary strength development, and, of course, proper diet and proper rest.

According to trainer Ken Johnson, "Strength exercises have nothing to do with oxygen. They make muscles and connective tissues stronger, they improve the flow of blood to the muscles, the muscle mass goes up, a number of things happen, but that doesn't necessarily involve anything in the way of aerobic benefit. You do get a minimal aerobic benefit from circuit weight training and Nautilus training, but that's not enough. You can get very good at at anaerobic exercises and not really benefit your heart and lungs. The opposite is true of aerobics. You can get quite good at them in terms of processing oxygen and delivering it to the tissues, and not do a whole lot in terms of general overall body strength. So each of the forms of exercise has major assets and liabilities. I think the main thing that's important is that the people who are consuming exercise as a real commodity around the country are looking now for a combination of things that will be good for them internally as well as things that will make them look good. That makes a lot of sense. The prisoner of war look is not in, so some of the positions taken by the fathers and mothers of the running movement have been modified; they now realize that you need a certain amount of strength training to go along with your aerobics, and vice versa, along with some flexibility work, or over the long term you're in deep trouble. You just won't operate as well."

There are a number of questions that anyone interested in defining and following a training regimen should ask and answer before taking the first deep knee-bend. According to Johnson, "First, take a critical look at yourself in a full-lengh mirror and say 'okay, this is where I am right now.' Then form a picture of yourself in your mind of what you'd realistically like to look like. Decide what you'd like to accomplish both short term—'I want to stop smoking,' or 'I want to drop 10 pounds,' or 'I'd like to fit into a certain suit'—and long term. Be specific. And then decide how much time each day you can commit to the effort. Be minimal in your commitment. Then consider what's available in terms of facilities and instruction in your area—are you going to do it on your own, use a health club or a personal trainer, work out with a friend, or base your program on existing exercise and work-out books. And the cost. All those details."

Then you're ready to begin. And you should begin as though you have fifty years to get where you're going. We all crawled before we walked and walked before we ran. And a steady progression is still necessary for an adult who's decided to get into shape.

ONE DAY AT A TIME

"I insist that everyone talk with his physician," says Johnson. "He or she can give you an idea of what kind of an operating pulse rate, or a safe working pulse rate, you can handle. Your doctor can show you how to take it. Use that pulse rate as a guideline. Whether you're walking or riding a bike or playing squash or skipping rope or swimming, it's the same measure. It's really the tachometer that tells you whether you're working below, at, or above, your recommended level of exertion.

"I then suggest to nearly everyone that they look at recreational walking with an eye toward making that the foundation from which everything else will sprout. It stretches the body out, it protects the bones and joints from all sorts of percussions, it will tone muscles, and it will cause a change in fat and muscle distribution. With from fifteen to twenty minutes of brisk walking at three to four miles an hour (a rate manageable by anyone but a cardiac patient) for four to five days a week, without really changing anything else in your daily routine, most people discover that they've lost six to eight pounds during the first month. That's how effective it is. It is a good user of calories.

"You should also begin to layer on calisthenics during the early stages of the program—exercises that use body weight as the opposable stress that allows your muscles, joints, and tendons to function more efficiently. Nautilus or Universal systems or fixed weights are things that should come later.

"A lot of people aren't in shape for walking, and they start running. Running may have been natural when you were a child but twenty and thirty years later, after you've stopped doing it, it isn't natural anymore. The lever muscles don't work the way they used to. You're carrying more weight, and your posture's not so great. So if you don't do some walking first, you're going to have trouble. The odds are good that you'll be an ex-jogger within a week.

SECOND THINGS SECOND

"After four to six weeks of walking and calisthenics and stretching (and of course trying to monitor your diet—nobody who's smart recommends making drastic dietary alterations at the same time as you start a program of exercise; it just dooms you to failure), it's reasonable to start thinking in terms of increasing the level of stress placed on your body. You can do additional flexibility or stretching exercises designed to mobilize the joints, keeping in mind that doing the calisthenics properly and walking correctly will also do a lot to stretch the joints. You can increase the workload of the calisthenics by changing the movements or increasing the repetitions and cutting down on the rest period between efforts. You can increase the aerobic benefits by increasing the walking pace or by beginning to use a bit of a canter, then a jog. The whole effort should be aimed toward gradually increasing the demands placed upon your body by the combination of anaerobic, anerobic, and flexibility exercises. The demand should increase gradually so that after you've been at it for three to four months your routine takes the better part of forty minutes to an hour of constant effort, and you work up a sweat. The real point is that you're the only person who can decide when you should go after a little more stress. It's really very simple if you just listen to your body."

REAPPRAISAL

It is at this point, when you're becoming comfortable with an exercise and conditioning regimen and your body is responding to the demands put upon it, that you should decide to get someone who can serve as a guidepost for you as a trainer. It's easy to find a trainer, but it's not necessarily easy to find someone who's good for you. Trainers, whether they're on health club staffs or working independently, have varying levels of enthusiam, different personalities, and different levels of education. Pay attention to your reaction to the trainer as an individual. You have to talk to him, meet him, ask him questions, and find out who he is. Always keep in mind, when you're working with a trainer, that your case and your body is very different from anyone else he has worked with.

A trainer can give you guidelines. There are no magic work-outs. In order for an advanced program to be good for you, make sure that the trainer asks, "let's find out who you are, you tell me what you want." You have to be specific. Say "I'm a runner" or "I don't do anything" or "I really want to go to Nepal and climb mountains." You want and need a personalized program, not just a sheet of paper listing exercises that have been given to six hundred other people. Whether you're gaining or losing weight, trying to become more muscular or defined, or trying to become better at climbing mountains or running marathons, there are different combinations of training forms that have to be put together. You want to maximize the time you spend trying to get where you're going. The goal is to reach the level of fitness you'll need to do what you want to do when you're ready to do it. You have to define it, and then work on it.

STOPPING IS THE HARDEST THING TO DO

Dr. Lawrence Moorhouse, considered the grandfather of modern exercise physiology, has written extensively on the reversal of training effect. Simply stated, the more advanced an individual's conditioning routine is and has been at the time the person stops exercising, the more rapid that person's decline and return to the beginning level of conditioning will be. If you stop working out for between two and four weeks, regardless of your level of conditioning you will experience a very definite decline. Muscle masses begin to reduce, blood supply to the muscles dwindles, and the connective tissues within the muscles begin to minimize. Reversals take place because the body is geared to do only what it has to. Quite literally, if you don't use your conditioning by forcing your body to maintain a certain level of activity, you lose it.

"If you eat like a horse and exercise like a horse, you're going to look like a horse."
—MOHAMMED ALI

This potential for rapid reversal is perhaps the strongest reason for you not to aim at a level of fitness that exceeds what you need for the life that you lead—there's no point to cultivating fitness that you can't really use. You'll lose it rapidly if you cannot or do not continue to devote the time and energy needed to achieve and maintain the higher levels of conditioning.

BEFORE YOU BEGIN

To determine how hard you should exercise, calculate your Maximum Work Capacity (MWC)—the rate of your pulse when your heart is beating as fast as it can. To determine the maximum safe heart rate for your age, subtract your age from 220. The resulting number is your MWC. To determine your heart rate during an exercise session, take your pulse (at either your wrist or the carotid artery at the side of your neck, just below the ear) immediately after your aerobics workout. Count the beats for fifteen seconds and multiply by four. The result should be between 60 and 80 percent of your MCW. If it isn't at least 60 percent, you're not exercising hard enough and won't derive the full benefits of your aerobic exercises.

According to Ken Johnson, "If an NFL ball player, a veteran of ten years, is told without warning, 'that's it, no more football' and he stops, he will, if he doesn't go through the proper detraining in terms of diet and exercise, end up with severe health problems. He is a potential victim of both muscle atrophy and weight gain. And there can be all sorts of problems with cardiac tissue that's been used to incredible stresses during practice and games and is not being asked to exert itself any more. Heart muscle, like any muscle, will atrophy.

"In my experience," says Johnson, "if you're not a professional athlete, the middle of the road is the place to be. You can maintain that with the least amount of Herculean effort. People who come to me really want to do something because they know they're supposed to—they know they have to. And they'll buck and fight and kick and scream that they have to do more rather than less. All I try to do is spread the word that you have to do the appropriate amount to fit your lifestyle. There are levels of conditioning that are healthful and reasonable. But if you overdo it, you won't do yourself any long-term good."

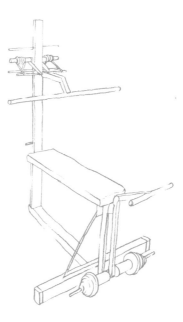

DEVELOPING A PROGRAM

Any exercise routine should begin with five minutes of warmup calisthenics to get the blood moving to your muscles and prepare them for more strenuous activity. This should be followed by strength-building exercises that concentrate on specific areas of the body—your arms, chest, back, abdomen, and legs. These strength builders can include calisthenics and weight training. Finally, you should include at least fifteen minutes of aerobic exercise—bicycling, running, swimming—to get your heart and lungs working.

The following exercises are good ones to include in any exercise program, although they're not all meant to be performed during every session. If, however, you're just beginning an exercise program, you should do all of the warmup exercise at the beginning of each session. After the warmups, begin with two or three of the conditioning exercises, which gradually become more strenuous. After exercising five times a week for two or three weeks, move on to more strenuous conditioning exercises and increase the duration of your work-out. Your body will let you know when you're ready to take on more.

WARMUP EXERCISES

1. *Bend and Stretch* (10 repetitions)
   1. Stand with your feet shoulder-width apart, arms at your sides.
   2. Bend forward and down, hands reaching for the floor. Flex your knees slightly and stretch gently to touch your toes.
   3. Return to the starting position.

2. *Knee Lift* (10 repetitions for each leg)
   1. Stand erect, arms at your sides.
   2. Raise your left knee as high as possible, pulling it against your body with both hands.
   3. Lower your foot to the floor and repeat with your right knee.

3. *Upper-body Stretch* (20 repetitions)
   1. Stand erect, fists clenched and elbows raised to shoulder height.
   2. Without arching your back, push both elbows back forcefully.
   3. Pull arms forward to the starting position.

4. *Half-knee Bend* (10 repetitions)
   1. Stand erect, hands on your hips.
   2. Bend knees into a gentle squat, simultaneously extending your arms, palms down, straight in front of you.
   3. Return to standing position.

5. *Arm Circles* (15 circles forward; then 15 circles back)
   1. Stand with your arms extended sideways at shoulder height, palms facing up.
   2. Draw small circles in the air with your fingertips, making sure to keep your arms straight at all times.

6. *Body Bender* (10 repetitions on each side)
   1. Stand with your feet apart, fingers interlaced behind your neck.
   2. Slowly bend your body sideways as far as you can, keeping your fingers locked behind your neck.
   3. Straighten up and repeat toward the other side.

CONDITIONING EXERCISES

1. *Prone Arch* (10 repetitions)
   1. Lie face down on the floor with your hands tucked under your thighs, palms up.
   2. Arching your back, slowly raise your head, shoulders, and legs from the floor. Then lower them slowly.

2. *Head and Shoulders Curl* (5 repetitions)
   1. Lie on your back with your hands tucked under the small of your back, palms down.
   2. Tense your stomach muscles and slowly raise only the upper half of your body—head, shoulders, and elbows —as high off the floor as you can.
   3. Hold that position for a count of four, then slowly lower yourself to the floor.

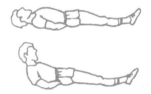

3. *Ankle Stretch* (15 repetitions)
   1. Stand on the edge of a stair or a thick book with your heels raised and all of your weight on the balls of your feet.
   2. Lower your heels. Pause, and raise them again.

4. *Toe Touch* (10 repetitions)
   1. Stand with your arms hanging comfortably at your sides.
   2. Bend forward, keeping your knees straight, and touch your fingertips to your ankles.
   3. Bounce down slightly and try to touch your toes. Stand up.

5. *Sprinter* (12 repetitions)
   1. Squat by bending your right knee and extending your left leg straight behind you. Lean forward so that both palms are flat on the floor, pointing straight ahead.
   2. In one bouncing motion, leaning your full weight on your hands, reverse leg positions by throwing your right foot back and bringing your left foot forward.
   3. Repeat.

6. *Sitting Stretch* (12 repetitions)
   1. Sit with your legs spread apart, your hands resting on your knees.
   2. Bend forward from the waist, reaching as far beyond your toes as you can.
   3. Sit up.

7. *Sit-up, Arms Extended* (5 repetitions)
   1. Lie on your back with your legs together and extended straight out. Your arms should be stretched straight out on the floor above your head.
   2. Keeping your arms straight, sit up and reach for your ankles.
   3. Grasp your ankles for a second, then let go and return to the starting position.

8. *Leg Raiser* (12 repetitions on each side)
   1. Lie on your right side, with your right arm extended over your head and your legs together.
   2. Raise your left leg about two feet off the floor, then slowly lower it back.
   3. Repeat 11 times on your right side, then roll over and begin on your left side.

9. *Push-up* (4 repetitions)
   1. Lie face down on the floor with your hands tucked
      under your shoulders, palms down, fingers pointing
      straight ahead.
   2. Push your body up and off the floor, your weight resting
      on your hands and toes, keeping your back straight.
      (Your buttocks should not be raised up in the air, and
      your abdomen should not sag down.)
   3. Lower your body to the floor.

10. *Flutter Kick* (30 repetitions)
    1. Lie face down on the floor with your hands tucked
       under your thighs, palms up.
    2. In a single motion, arch your back to raise your head,
       chest, and legs.
    3. Bend your knees slightly and kick a swimmer's flutter
       kick, counting each kick as one repetition. Make sure
       you kick from the hips.

11. *Sit-up, Fingers Laced* (12 repetitions)
    1. Lie on your back with your legs flat on the floor,
       spread apart. Lace your fingers behind your neck.
    2. Sit up slowly. Swivel your body, touching your right
       elbow to your left knee. Lie back down.
    3. Sit up again. Swivel your body, touching your left
       elbow to your right knee. Each sit-up counts as one.

12. *Sit-up, Fingers Laced, Knees Bent* (30 repetitions)
    1. Lie on your back with your knees bent and your fingers
       interlaced behind your neck. (It helps to have someone
       hold your feet or to anchor them under a piece of
       furniture.)
    2. Roll your body up to a sitting position, bringing your
       left elbow over to touch your right knee. Lie back
       down.
    3. Repeat, bringing your right elbow to your left knee.
       Each sit-up counts as one.

TO SUM UP...

- The keys to a healthy diet are moderation and variety.

- Low-calorie diets, during which you consume fewer calories than your body burns, are the most sensible choice for weight loss.

- Eat lightly. Substitute fish, chicken, turkey, or veal for red meat, and poach or broil foods rather than frying them.

- Avoid salt and sugar in any form.

- Learn to substitute, e.g., water for alcohol and fresh-cut vegetables for rich hors d'oeuvres.

- Look beyond "natural." Many foods labeled "natural" are high in salt and sugar and are, in fact, less healthful than some processed versions of the same foods. Check the labels.

- If you plan to consult a nutritionist, choose one who is registered with the American Dietetic Association in Chicago. Their telphone number is (312) 280-5000.

- Always perform warmup exercises to stretch and prepare your muscles before beginning more vigorous activities.

- Integrate the full range of exercise types into your fitness program: aerobics to tone the cardiovascular system and improve muscle tone; and anaerobics to help develop your muscle strength and flexibility.

- Check your pulse rate during your fitness routine to make sure that your body is receiving the maximum benefits offered by exercise.

- Patience is essential for any fitness program. You won't see results overnight, but they'll be worth waiting for.

WARDROBE

The look and the reality of men's fashions is a result of evolution, not, as much of the fashion press would have everyone believe, revolution. Over a period of years lapels widen slightly or narrow a bit, neckties (always in relation to lapels) gain in breadth or become a little skinnier, pants legs flare—and then taper. Admittedly, from time to time, certain looks, such as the leisure suit, seem to come upon us with the speed of a meteor, but these looks usually vanish almost as quickly. Fortunately, the inexorable evolution of the basic men's wardrobe is relatively slow and steady. It isn't necessary to adopt a new look overnight. Your wardrobe can evolve economically by replacing items as they wear out and adding new elements as your personal finances allow.

The dominant considerations are comfort and quality. Comfort—in that a two- or three-button grey flannel suit made of today's worsted flannel is light enough to be worn during all but the very hottest and very coldest days of the year—and quality, in that the linings, the set of the lapels, the detailing—buttons and pockets and linings and stitches—on better ready-made suits and jackets are similar to the details that just a few years ago were available on only the most expensive tailored garments.

A sense of personal style always involves comfort and quality. If you're not comfortable with what you're wearing, that discomfort is usually quite evident. Finding clothes and accessories that suit you involves both self-analysis and trial and error. "It requires a great sense of honesty," observes Geoffrey Beene, "in that you must identify your good points or bad points and play them up or down accordingly. I always think of the time Winston Churchill said, 'If you wear glasses, make a point of your wearing glasses.' He wore glasses with big black rims. And he demonstrated that an exaggerated look can fit into someone's personal style."

Defining your clothing style is rewarding because it allows you to relax and enjoy clothing rather than being distracted by it. In building or expanding a wardrobe, the particular cut and coloration of a suit, a jacket, a pair of trousers, or a necktie, although based upon broad standards, are individual decisions influenced by where you live, your business and social requirements, and your personal taste. No one can dictate these decisions to you. Although the pages that follow consider some guidelines, the focus is on recognizing quality in order to get the most from your clothing investment. Choosing wisely and then caring well for the many items that make up a wardrobe are the basis for accomplishing this.

"Above all, clothing should be a pleasure, not a source of worry. What you wear should simply allow you to enjoy yourself more by helping you look and feel on top of every situation."
EGON VON FÜRSTENBERG,
The Power Look

THE SILHOUETTES

There are three primary suit styles that bear consideration. In the trade, the cut or look of a suit is called the "silhouette," and the three leading styles—the European, the Sack (or Brooks Brothers Natural-Shoulder suit), and the American—offer markedly different silhouettes.

THE EUROPEAN CUT

The *European cut* is an extremely stylized silhouette. The shoulders are padded and distinct. The armholes, fitted closely to the body, are high, and offer little excess space for moving the upper arm. The jacket tapers radically at the waist and the pant leg is narrow.

European Cut Double-Breasted Jacket

European Cut Single-Breasted Jacket

THE SACK

The *Sack*, also called the Brooks Brothers Natural-Shoulder suit, is, as its name indicates, cut loosely and with little taper in the jacket waist. The naturally shaped, unpadded shoulders appear narrow, the jacket features three or four buttons, flapped side pockets, and a single vent. The trousers are more fully cut than on the American silhouette and fall straight along the leg.

The Sack

The American Cut

THE AMERICAN CUT

The *American cut*, the most comfortable of the three, is a synthesis of the best qualities of both the Sack and the European styles. It has naturally sloping shoulders with an armhole large enough to make movement relatively fluid and easy. The jacket shapes to the body and has a slightly tapered waist, accenting the body line but not dictating it. The jacket, usually with two buttons, occasionally three, has a tapered lapel and is shaped to be held together by the top button if there are two buttons, the middle button if there are three. The trousers fall straight along the leg, measuring approximately nineteen to nineteen and a half inches at the knee and carrying this width down to the base.

CHOICES

It's important to decide which look best complements your body and your lifestyle. "Any piece of clothing is of no value," says Geoffrey Beene, "if it does not function, if you're not comfortable in it, or if it doesn't fill the needs and expectations of a particular situation. Clothes have to be wearable." Beene points to the 1960s "peacock period" in menswear as an example of unwearable clothing. "It didn't work," he says. "There were European-style suits with armholes cut so high you couldn't move in them. The clothes had no validity, because they defied the body."

You also have the choice of ready-to-wear, semi-custom-made, or custom-made suits. While a custom-made, or even semi-custom-made, suit is undeniably more luxurious than the ready-made variety, few men can afford a wardrobe composed entirely of custom-made suits. That's not a tragedy. A well-designed, well-made, properly fitted off-the-rack suit constructed of good fabric can look as good and wear as well as its custom-tailored counterparts. A custom-made suit is fitted to your body piece by piece during a series of fittings with a tailor. A semi-custom-made suit is cut from a standard pattern and then altered to accommodate your measurements before the suit is assembled. Additional alterations are made after the suit is sewn. A ready-to-wear or off-the-rack suit comes in a variety of standard sizes, and alterations are made to improve its fit after you've bought it.

"It's a mistake for a man to wear something just because it's fashionable. If the clothing you're wearing is right for you, you won't want to loosen your tie or collar or take off your jacket the first chance you get. I've always thought that Fred Astaire and Cary Grant are good examples of style—they're always well-dressed, but they also look extremely comfortable in their clothing."

—TOM CONWAY

"There used to be numerical grades given to ready-made suits," says Stanley Tucker, executive vice president of Geoffrey Beene, Inc. "The grades were based on the number of minutes of hand tailoring that went into the suit's production. Grade six was the best and most expensive. It included suits made by Hickey/Freeman and Oxxford, which feature a great deal of handwork—the lapels may be hand-stitched, the buttonholes were probably done by hand, and the buttons may have been placed by hand . Grade four, which was second best, was a perfectly respectable suit that had some handwork. Grade two had an absolute minimum of handwork. And more recently some manufacturers produced a grade X, which is lower than grade two. Human hands never touched an X suit—it virtually flew through the machines in the factory. The grades aren't used any more, but the standards still apply."

LOOKING FOR QUALITY

Before you choose a suit, check its workmanship and fiber content. By law, the label must list the fabric used in the suit. Natural fibers, such as cotton, linen, and wool, look and feel better than synthetic fabrics, but they are more delicate and require careful care and handling. Synthetic fabrics last longer. A blend of the two, such as 60 percent wool to 40 percent polyester, is a practical combination of both fabric's good qualities.

Quality Checks: The Jacket
It's important that the lapels are set properly. They should gently roll onto the jacket, without looking pressed in. The stitches around the edges of the lapels should be unobtrusive—small and neatly spaced.

Check the stitches that attach the collar to the jacket as well. They too should be small and and regular, but not perfectly even, which would indicate machine stitching.

Generous use of fabric as shown at the inseams is another hallmark of a good garment. There should be at least two to three inches inside the back and side seams of a jacket so that it can easily be let out if necessary.

Pay attention to the lining. A good jacket will be fully lined, usually with silk or rayon. The sleeve lining should be attached securely to the body of the lining at the armhole, and should extend all the way to the cuff of the jacket. (Summer-weight jackets are an exception —they may be only half-lined for comfort, to allow the jacket to "breathe.")

The interior pockets should be comfortably placed and not bulge unnecessarily when used. The major pockets on better suits have buttons and loop clasps that offer added protection when you're carrying a wallet or important papers.

Much of the body and shape of the jacket come from the interlining used in the lapels, chest, and shoulders. Squeeze the lapels—if they have enough interlining, they'll spring right back into shape. Some jackets are fused, some have a floating chest piece. If a coat is fused (the lining is in effect laminated to the suit fabric), with frequent dry cleaning the lining pad will begin to show through and the jacket will show a warp. This is because the lining and the main fabric react to cleaning chemicals and heat differently and tighten at different rates. It doesn't take much heat to cause this.

Check the buttons. Plastic buttons will crack sooner or later, so look for buttons that are at least partially made of bone or pearl. If the button is not clear through and has a slightly darker color on the back, then it contains bone, pearl, or shell. These last longer than an all-plastic button. Make sure the buttons are securely sewn (better suits will have a couple of spare buttons sewn to the inside of the jacket).

SHOPPING

Define what you're looking for before you arrive at the store. You'll get much more help from the salesman if you can tell him whether you want an American or European cut, trousers with or without cuffs, pockets with or without flaps, and the approximate color and fabric weight you're looking for. You won't have to waste his time— or yours—looking at suits that aren't close to what you want.

POCKET STYLES

A *flap pocket* has a flap of material covering its opening.

A *besom pocket*, usually inside the suit, has no flap.

A *patch pocket* is formed by stitching a piece of suiting material to the outside of the suit.

Ideally, you should shop for suits and jackets while wearing what you consider to be your best-fitting suit, a belt, and the shoes—or at least the type of shoes—you expect to wear with the clothes you're buying. If you usually wear shirts with French cuffs, wear one on the shopping trip, and wear the sort of tie you would normally wear to work. Carry your eyeglasses, keys, cigarettes, wallet—all the things you'd normally put in your pockets to see how they fit into the new suit or jacket.

Once the salesman shows you where to find the the size and style of suit you're interested in, ask him to leave you alone while you look. You can't make a studied decision if you feel at all pressured. "A salesman may hold or adjust part of the suit as you look in the mirror and tell you it looks terrific," says Tucker. "Tell him to get away from you. You have to turn around, button the jacket, unbutton it, take it off, and put it on again. That's the only way you'll be able to tell if it really fits you."

If you see a suit you like on the rack, try on the jacket. If it seems a bit too tight or too loose, don't hesitate to try on a different size. A size 40 by one manufacturer may be a 42 by another. Sizing is dictated by the "drop," the difference between the chest measurement of the jacket and the waist measurement of the pants. Traditional clothing has a six-inch drop, which means a 40-regular suit will have trousers with a 34-inch waist. Recently, however, some manufacturers have begun to pay attention to the more athletic body, so they cut with a seven-inch to a ten-inch drop, which means that a 40-regular suit may have trousers with a 33- or even a 30-inch waist. And some manufacturers cut their clothing for a heavier body—a few manufacturers offer suits with as little as a four-inch drop. And, of course, the cut of the jacket varies slightly as well.

THE CHANGING ROOM

When you find a jacket that fits and looks well on you, go to the fitting room to try on the trousers. Fill the pockets with all the things you normally carry. The tailor can thus take this into consideration before he begins work on your jacket. But never stuff the pockets of any garment—you'll ruin the lines.

As you try on clothes, make sure to retain your natural posture. A tailor may tell you to stand up straight, but don't take on an unnatural stance—you want the suit to fit you, the way you normally are.

A WELL-FITTING JACKET

A properly made suit is a blend of elegance and comfort. The jacket should be loose enough across the shoulders to allow you to move your arms freely, but not so loose that the lapels sag in front.

The collar should lie flat against the back of your neck with about half an inch of shirt collar showing above it. Ridges or puckers at the back of the jacket mean that it doesn't fit and probably never will, even with alterations. Try another.

Study the shoulders carefully. Some jackets aren't evenly balanced, which makes the whole suit look lopsided and awkward.

The proper jacket sleeve stops about five inches from the base of your thumb, revealing approximately half an inch of shirt cuff. To check a sleeve's length, allow your shoulders to follow their natural pitch. Don't stand ramrod stiff with your shoulders held rigidly up and back unless that's your normal posture; it will give you a false picture.

To determine the proper length of the jacket skirt, let your arms hang comfortably by your sides and curl your hands. The hem of the jacket should fit into that curl.

A suit or jacket that creases easily will have to be pressed frequently, taking months off its normal lifespan. To find out if a fabric will wrinkle excessively, twist the jacket's sleeve hard for twelve to fifteen seconds, then let it go. If the sleeve springs back without a wrinkle, the suit will wear well.

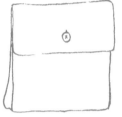

A *bellows pocket* has a pleat that expands, allowing the pocket to hold more.

A *hacking pocket* is a flap pocket set at an angle to accentuate the suit's lines.

WELL-FITTING TROUSERS

The waistband should be reinforced (curtained or at least half-cur-tained) to keep it from rolling over the top of your belt. There should be a second button on the inside of the waist to the left of the fly. This takes strain away from the main waist button and gives a flatter look and a better fit. The waist of the trousers should rest slightly below your navel, and there should be just enough room for you to slip the flat of your hand between you and the waistband.

Reinforced Waistband

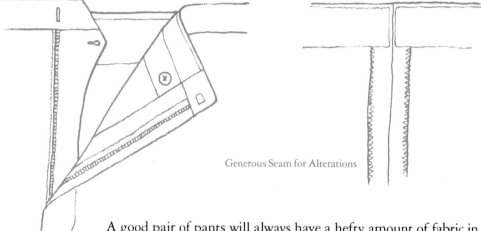

Generous Seam for Alterations

A good pair of pants will always have a hefty amount of fabric in the inseam, to permit alterations. Excess fabric should be available all the way down from the waistband through the crotch.

A good pair of pants will be half lined, from the upper thigh to a point three to four inches below the knee. The lining keeps the knee from bulging out when you've been sitting. And it feels good. The trousers' fit is dictated by its "rise"—the distance from the center point of the crotch to the top of the waistband. The normal rise nowadays is approximately ten and a half inches. Low-rise pants are normally for younger people, because they fit more tightly. Jeans, for instance, normally have a rise of eight to nine inches. Trousers should fit smoothly—not tightly—all the way down to the hems, which should just brush the top of your shoes and hang one-half to one inch longer in the back than they do in the front. If the trousers have cuffs, they should be even all the way around.

After the tailor has pinned the alterations in place, move around in the trousers. Sit, bend, and walk around a bit, watching yourself in the mirror. If the trousers still look and feel good, buy the suit.

A WELL-FITTING VEST

A matching—or even contrasting—vest can add a finishing touch to a suit or to trousers and a sport coat. Vests should not add any bulk to your overall look—they should lie smoothly over your shirt and fit easily under your jacket. Vests are traditionally worn with the bottom button unfastened—a custom that dates back to the days of Beau Brummel.

"Clothing is very much like fragrance; it's like a second skin. Therefore, it becomes very emotional."
—GEOFFREY BEENE

DOUBLE-CHECK ALTERATIONS

Always try the suit on again after the alterations have been made. Check carefully in a mirror to make sure all the alterations have been done to your satisfaction, and to see if the suit needs any additional work. If you're not completely satisfied, ask that the necessary work be done before you accept the suit. If the store refuses, get your money back and leave the suit behind. If a store can't or won't provide you with a suit that fits, it doesn't deserve your business.

BLAZERS AND SPORT JACKETS

Blazers and sport jackets, worn with casual trousers, or sometimes even jeans, are acceptable attire for many situations.

A blazer should be a staple of any wardrobe. Designed in 1850 by the captain of the H.M.S *Blazer* as a uniform for his crew, the blazer is one of the most versatile and flattering jackets available. Although blazers are made in many colors, the traditional navy blue version with gold or silver buttons is by far the most distinguished. Choose a lightweight wool or wool-blend blazer for year-round wear. If you're buying a sport jacket for casual business wear, you'll want to choose a conservative color and cut. If you're planning to wear it only during your leisure time, you'll have more freedom of choice.

Single-Breasted Blazer

Sport Jacket

A sport jacket is very much like a blazer but is usually cut about an inch longer. When choosing either a sport jacket or blazer, remember that each should be fitted as carefully as a suit jacket. Check the workmanship, see that the collar and lapels lie flat, and make sure that you can move your arms and body freely.

Both blazers and sport jackets can be brushed as you would brush a suit jacket (see page 80).

JEANS AND TROUSERS

When buying trousers to wear with jackets and blazers, remember that color is the key to getting the most out of your investment. Rich, solid colors—blue, grey, and tan—are most likely to coordinate well with the rest of your wardrobe. Dress and casual slacks are sometimes interchangeable, and should definitely be altered to fit as you would have suit trousers altered. Usually, however, there are subtle differences in the fit of each.

Dress trousers are generally fitted exactly like suit trousers. They fit high on the waist, the waistband resting just below the navel. They tend to have very conservative features, such as unobtrusive, vertically cut pockets, and little or no detailing. A good pair of dress trousers will be displayed unfinished; the length of the leg and the style of the hem need to be adjusted by the store's tailor.

Casual trousers tend to rest lower on the body than suit or dress trousers, the waistband sitting a little above the hips. Pockets are an important detail on many casual trousers, which may have patch pockets, flap pockets, or buttoned pockets on the front or the back.

Jeans, of denim, corduroy, or other fabrics, are comfortable and durable casual trousers, available in many weights and styles. Once a part of the wardrobe of laborers and later adopted by the counterculture, jeans are now worn, at least on weekends, by almost everybody. Finding well-fitting jeans can take a little time because all manufacturers cut them slightly differently. Jeans should fit close to the body, but not so tight that it's a struggle to get into them, as was the case with the designer-jeans fad of a few years ago. Try several kinds until you find a model and size that look well on you. Once you've made up your mind, try on two or three pairs of the same make and size—chances are that each will fit slightly differently. It's a good idea to buy jeans that are slightly long for you. Although most are pre-shrunk by the manufacturer, they may still shrink a bit in length after the first washing.

Although many men like the look of faded denims (in fact, you can buy "prefaded" jeans, or a special packet of bleach to toss in the wash so they fade the first time they're laundered), you can retain their dark, crisp look longer by washing them inside out in cold water.

FORMAL WEAR

The standard black *tuxedo*, with satin lapels and a strip of satin along the outer seams of the trousers, is always correct for any formal occasion. If you attend three or more black-tie events a year, buy your own tuxedo. A custom-fitted tuxedo will always look more distinguished than a rented one, which is unlikely to conform to your contours as well as it should. Properly cared for, a well-made tuxedo will last at least ten years—as long as you haven't bought a "trendy" one that quickly looks dated. Choose a fabric that can be worn comfortably year-round—lightweight wool, linen, or silk are your best choices.

If you don't attend many formal events and would rather not rent a tuxedo, a simple, elegantly cut black suit, worn with a white shirt and a black bow tie, will suffice.

Once you've selected an elegant-looking tuxedo, choose its accessories as carefully. The classic *tuxedo shirt* is made of finely woven white linen and has crisp vertical pleats on the chest. Avoid ruffled, pastel dress shirts—they can't compare to the simple, striking white shirt.

The correct *bow tie* is black satin or silk, although velvet is also acceptable. If you're short and thin, choose a narrow bow tie; larger men can wear the more elaborate "butterfly" bow ties.

You can wear a black *cummerbund* with its pleats facing up (a tradition stemming from the days when the pleats were intended to catch crumbs dropped in the course of a formal dinner); or a black satin *waistcoat*—a formal vest that has a strap instead of a back, making it more comfortable to wear under a jacket.

> *"Lightweight fabrics are very important in men's clothes, especially in formal wear. Let's face it, most rooms are designed, temperature-wise, for a woman wearing a backless dress."*
> —ROBERT KELLY

Footwear is important for completing the formal look—*sheer black silk hose* with *patent leather pumps* are traditional, although you can get by with a simple pair of well-shined black shoes.

The black *Chesterfield* coat is the most appropriate choice for wear with formal wear, but any dark overcoat or trench coat will do. Dress up the coat by draping a white or cream colored silk scarf around your neck.

FABRICS FOUND IN SUITS, JACKETS, VESTS, AND TROUSERS

Bedford Cloth is a ribbed fabric made of wool, silk, cotton, synthetic, or blended fibers. It can be identified by a distinct rib that runs the length of the fabric.

Corduroy is a strong, casual-looking ribbed fabric made from cotton or a cotton blend.

Denim is a sturdy fabric woven from cotton or a cotton blend, characterized by colored threads running across the fabric and white threads running its length.

Drill is a durable fabric woven from cotton or cotton blends.

Flannel, made from cotton or wool, is a soft fabric woven into a variety of weights.

Gabardine is a a tightly woven fabric made of cotton or wool. (It may occasionally contain blends of polyester or rayon.) It is strong and holds its shape well.

Harris Tweed is the trade name for a sturdy woolen fabric that has been dyed, spun, and handwoven on Harris or one of the other islands of the Outer Hebrides off the coast of northern Scotland.

Hopsacking, made of cotton, linen, or rayon, has a slightly rough surface.

Linen, popular in summer-weight suits, is derived from the stalk of the flax plant. It breathes well and is comfortable to wear. Because they're made from a fairly stiff fiber, linen garments tend to wear quickly at edges and folds. Like cotton clothes, they can shrink, and they wrinkle easily. "Americans are just starting to understand linen," says Ralph DiNapoli, the men's suit buyer for Bloomingdale's main office in Manhattan. "They now realize that you wear it wrinkled—that it's supposed to look that way." Don't attempt to launder linen suits yourself—they'll lose their shape.

Poplin, made from cotton, is a smooth fabric with a fine rib running across its surface.

Seersucker, a lightweight cotton or cotton-synthetic blend, has an irregular, puckered surface that results from alternating the tension of yarns during the weaving process.

Silk, a protein-based fiber found in the cocoon of the silk worm, is surprisingly strong and versatile. Silk fabrics, available in many weights, are warm, absorbent, and nearly immune to moths, mildew, and wrinkling. Silk requires very special care—it can be weakened by exposure to direct sunlight and perspiration. It must be dry cleaned.

Serge, made from wool, cotton, or cotton blends, is crisp-looking and tailors well.

Sharkskin is produced by weaving a white wool yarn with another color, usually black, brown, or blue.

Tweed, a rough-surfaced woolen fabric, derives its distinctive coloring from fiber dyeing.

Wool, a protein-based fiber taken from the coats of goats and sheep, is available in a variety of weights. It lends itself especially well to tailoring and is durable and naturally wrinkle-resistant. Brushing will keep wool suits looking good between infrequent dry cleanings.

CARING FOR SUITS, JACKETS, VESTS, AND TROUSERS

A few minutes of care each time you wear a garment will guarantee that it will look its best the next time you want to wear it.

Don't get into the habit of handling your clothes carelessly, then sending them to the dry cleaners to have them cleaned and pressed to repair the damage you've done. Suits should be dry cleaned as infrequently as possible (ideally no more than once or twice during a season) because the chemicals used in the dry-cleaning process will inevitably damage the fabric and shorten its lifespan. When you feel your suit needs to be professionally pressed, talk to your dry cleaner. Ask if he's equipped to do steam air finishing, in which the suit is placed on a form and steamed. If he can't, then specify a light pressing. With these precautions, a flannel worsted suit can last for ten years.

You won't have to visit the dry cleaner often if you care for your clothes properly at home. One of the simplest, but one of the most crucial, elements of suit care is storage.

"You don't wear out your suits by wearing them back and forth to work. You kill your suits when you start laying around the house in them, really crumbling them up. Then they have to be cleaned and pressed, and that's what hurts them."
—FRANK GIAMBRONE,
Senior executive vice president, sales,
Jacqueline Cochran, Inc.

Even if a suit is creased from a day's wear, the creases will fall out if you hang it up while it's still warm from your body. Empty your pockets first—the weight of keys and coins can pull the pockets out of shape. Don't put it back in the closet right away—hook the hanger over a shower rod or the top of a door and give the suit a good airing first to eliminate stale odors. While the suit is airing, brush it to remove lint and dust.

TO BRUSH A JACKET

Use a natural-bristle clothes brush to stroke the fabric briskly, concentrating on the folds and crevices where dust gathers. Don't jab or scrub the suit with the brush—you run the risk of tearing and wearing the fabric. Instead, brush up the nap to remove dust, then brush downward to smooth the finish. You can freshen heavy winter suits this way if you dip the bristles of the brush into a bowl of water with a few drops of ammonia added.

1. Turn out the collar to brush its interfacing, then turn it back down and brush the outside.

2. Brush the shoulders. With the jacket lining facing you, put your left hand inside one shoulder with your palm facing downward. Spread your fingers and curl them to the shape of the shoulder. The jacket's shoulder should lie on the back of your hand.

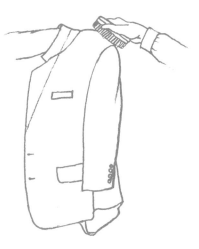

3. Use your other hand to brush down the nap from the inside edge of the collar to the outside edge of the shoulder.

4. Brush the front of the sleeve from shoulder to cuff.

5. Brush the second shoulder and sleeve as described in steps 2, 3, and 4.

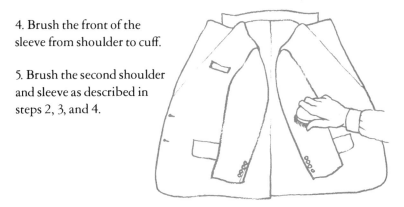

6. Fold both sleeves forward and brush their backs, sweeping the brush up and down the nap. Don't forget to brush inside and outside the cuffs.

7. Brush the back of the jacket upward from hem to collar, then downward from collar to hem.

8. To brush the front of the jacket, turn up the collar and lapels so that you can brush underneath them. Sweep the brush from the hem to the shoulders and then brush back down again to the hem.

9. Brush between the buttons.

10. Turn down the lapels and brush them.

TO BRUSH TROUSERS

1. If the trousers have cuffs, turn the cuffs down and brush out the dust that gets kicked into them.

2. Using long sweeping strokes, brush the front and then the back of each leg from hem to waistband.

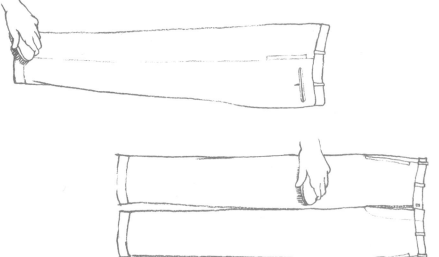

3. Smooth the finish by
brushing the front and then
the back of each leg from
waistband to hem.

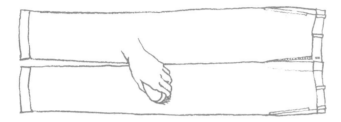

HANGING A SUIT

Once a suit has been aired and brushed, it's ready to be put in the
closet. Make sure it's on a wooden, plastic, or padded hanger—the
wire ones rust and can leave a thin ridge in the shoulder.

Double-barred wooden hangers are a good choice because they're
sturdy enough to hold a heavy suit, and plastic or wooden wishbone
hangers, curved to approximate the contours of your shoulders and
back, are good for keeping jackets in shape.

No matter what kind of hanger you're using, it should never extend
beyond the jacket's shoulder or it will poke into the arm, leaving a
ridge in the sleeve.

To hang a suit on a double-barred hanger, remove the belt from the
trousers and hang them over the bottom bar, taking care to see that
they are centered over the bar and both legs are lying smoothly, one
directly above the other, to avoid creases. The ankles and waist
should be evenly balanced, so the portion about six inches above
the knees should be draped over the bar. (Since the knees get the
most wear, you don't want to add to it by hanging the knee portion
over the bar.) When hanging two pairs of trousers on a hanger,
drape them in opposite directions so that the legs of each pair hang
from opposite sides of the bar.

If the suit has a vest, hang that up first, then put the jacket over it facing the same way. The center of the collar should rest squarely against the crook of the hanger and the shoulders should sit evenly so that the jacket hangs straight. Leave the vest and jacket open to allow air to circulate in and around them.

IRONING

If your suit does retain some creases after you've worn it a few times, you can press out the creases by ironing only those places on the suit that need it. Like dry cleaning, ironing causes wear and tear on clothes and shouldn't be overdone. Follow these guidelines:

Iron Temperatures

HOT *(210° C/410°F)*
Cotton, linen,
and rayon.

WARM *(160° C/320°F)*
Polyester
and wool.

COOL *(120° C/184°F)*
Acrylic, nylon,
acetate, and
triacetate.

Wools, Tweeds, and Heavy Suitings

Sturdy fabrics require a very hot iron combined with a damp cloth placed on the outside of the fabric to generate the steam required to open strong fibers and smooth creases. A large linen handkerchief or thin tea towel make good pressing cloths. Either wet the cloth thoroughly and wring it out until it's nearly dry, or dampen it slightly as you work with a spray mister (the kind used to water plants). Lay the damp cloth against the right side of the fabric in the area you're ironing and place the iron on top of it, always keeping the iron moving to avoid scorching the garment.

Cottons, Linens, Silks, and Delicate Suitings

Cotton, linen, and silk can all be pressed on the right side through a damp cloth. Cotton and linen require a hot (210°C/410°F) iron. A steamer, rather than an iron, is the best choice for gently removing creases from silk and very fine fabrics. If you don't have a steamer, you can iron them with a warm (160°C/320°F) iron.

Corduroy

Mist the fabric so it's slightly damp, then smooth it in the direction of the nap with a cloth. Press with a warm iron.

IRONING SUITS

Don't iron the entire suit unless it's absolutely necessary. Jackets tend to crease at the elbow and down the back, and you can eliminate these creases without doing the rest of the jacket.

When just the lining is wrinkled, turn the jacket inside out and hang it near a boiling kettle or near a steaming shower. If you do need to iron the entire garment periodically, do it according to the steps below.

Jacket

1. Lay the unbuttoned jacket, lining side down, on an ironing board or table protected by a blanket. Fold the lapels out so they lie flat against the ironing surface.

2. Press the lapels from just above the buttons and buttonholes to just beyond the V where they join the collar. (Don't press the collar itself—it's not supposed to have a sharp crease.)

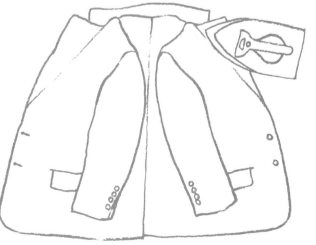

3. Turn the jacket over and iron directly onto the lining. (Mist silk linings lightly with water before you iron them.) Push the vents aside and iron the back flap. You can iron the vents if they need it, but they don't usually wrinkle much.

4. Fold in the jacket's sides and lay the first sleeve flat. Press the sleeve through a dampened cloth.

5. Press the second sleeve.

6. Turn the arms of the jacket inside out, and hold a clothes brush under one shoulder to support it and protect your hand from the iron's heat. Hold the brush so that the material lies over the bristles and the handle presses into the palm of your hand. Use a spray mister to dampen the lining, then iron directly on it.

7. Iron the other shoulder.

8. For a professional finish, hang the jacket where you can reach around it easily. You can use a steamer on it or wrap a damp cloth around an iron. Start with the cuffs, putting a clothes brush inside the first cuff (bristles facing outward) and lightly touching the creases with the steamer or iron. Gently touch up any creases that remain on the front or back of the jacket.

Vest

The lining at the back creases easily, but it takes only a moment or two to press.

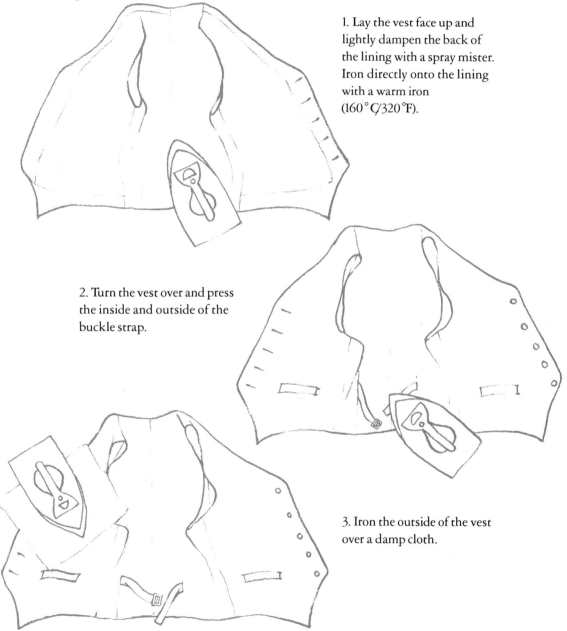

1. Lay the vest face up and lightly dampen the back of the lining with a spray mister. Iron directly onto the lining with a warm iron (160°C/320°F).

2. Turn the vest over and press the inside and outside of the buckle strap.

3. Iron the outside of the vest over a damp cloth.

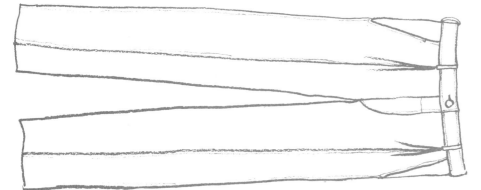

Trousers

You can press in a sharp, professional-looking front crease yourself. To position the crease properly, pick up the pants by the cuffs and line up all four seams. The front and back creases on each leg should fall halfway between the seams.

You can also iron jeans following the steps below. Just turn them inside out before you begin and brush them gently when you've finished to soften the fabric.

1. Lay the trousers on the ironing surface with the front creases nearest you. (You'll only have to iron the inseam of each leg—the warmth will penetrate both sides. Jeans are an exception; they need both sides of the leg pressed.)

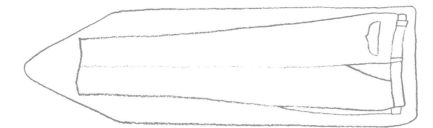

2. Fold the top leg back from the leg underneath. If the trousers are lined, make sure the lining lies flat. Smooth the bottom leg and lay a dampened cloth over the top portion of the front crease.

3. Press along the crease from waistband to cuffs by spraying the cloth, sliding the iron over the damp patch three or four times until the steam disappears, them moving down the crease and

repeating. As you move the hot iron along the crease, pull the cloth back frequently to make sure that you're not accidentally creating more than one crease.

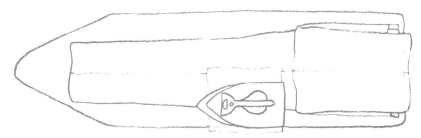

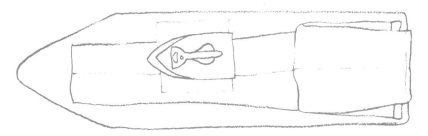

4. Turn the pants over, fold back the ironed leg, and iron the second leg as you did the first.

5. Lightly iron the seat and front of the trousers, following their natural contours.

SHIRTS

Shirts are available in an array of fabrics—cottons, synthetics, and blends of both. Cottons, chiefly broadcloth and oxford cloth, are cool, comfortable, and unquestionably better looking than synthetics, but they also cost more, and shrink and wrinkle more easily. Synthetics won't shrink and will resist creases. If you send your shirts out to be professionally laundered and pressed, the extra care and constant ironing that superior cotton shirts need shouldn't concern you. If you care for them yourself, however, you'll probably want to choose shirts that are a blend of cotton and synthetic fibers, to give you the beauty and comfort of cotton and the practical aspects of synthetics. If you do choose blend, always look for "reverse blends"—fabrics that contain more natural fiber than synthetic fiber. A 70/30, 60/40, or 55/45 ratio of cotton to synthetic are all good choices.

"Buying dress shirts is primarily a matter of common sense. Feel the fabric—you don't have to be an expert to tell if it feels harsh or smooth. Harsh fabric is poorly made and won't hold up."
—NORA HOLLEY, *Bloomingdale's*

"Natural fibers and high-quality fabrics allow for a clarity of color and subtlety of pattern that synthetics and blends just can't give you," says Nora Holley, the men's dress-shirt buyer for Bloomingdale's in New York. "I would not advise a customer to buy blends unless he does his own shirts. If he does his own, you don't want to sentence him to permanent ironing. But if you send your shirts out, a cotton, or any natural fiber, shirt will last far longer and hold its color better."

Oxford cloth and broadcloth are the two basic types of natural shirt fabrics. Oxford tends to be a denser weave, but pinpoint oxford, which is becoming very popular, is made with a weaving process that makes it feel almost silky. It's the most expensive oxford cloth—a pinpoint oxford shirt costs around $45.

The first thing to look for in a shirt is the way the fabric feels. If it's harsh, it's probably been woven cheaply, using fewer threads per inch, which makes it feel rough and unpleasant. In a broadcloth, the better the fabric, the silkier it feels.

If the shirt is pinned anywhere, pull a pin out. A good, dense fabric will always reweave itself immediately and the tiny hole will disappear. If the fabric is of a poor quality, that hole will stay for a long time.

There are many qualities of broadcloth. The top of the line is Sea Island cotton, which used to be produced in Sea Island, Georgia, although it's now made in Japan. It's made from a superior and rare cotton plant, and if you didn't know it was cotton you'd think it was silk. The typical Sea Island cotton shirt probably has thirty threads per inch, and costs between $75 and $140.

You can tell a lot about a shirt without ever taking it out of the package. A quality shirt will be in a "soft pack," with absolutely no cardboard. The shirt is surrounded only by tissue. Cheaper shirts are packed with cardboard because they'll be placed on a selling floor and handled by dozens of people. The shirt and package have to be durable. A fine shirt, however, will be kept behind a counter and a salesperson will hand it to you if you're interested in it.

Look at how the collar is set in the shirt. If it looks bad in the package, it's going to look bad when you wear it. The stitches on the collar should be small and flat. An average to moderately priced shirt will have sixteen or eighteen threads per inch; a very good shirt should have twenty-two to twenty-six threads per inch. You don't have to count them—you can tell just by looking at how close together they are. The buttons should be cross-stitched and made of pearl or bone, which won't crack. An all-plastic button will be clear all the way through; a bone or pearl button will be a little darker in the back.

"In shirts, you get what you pay for. If you're buying a designer shirt, unlike many other designer items, it's very rare that you're paying only for the name. Generally, the designer shirt is made of high-quality fabric and is well constructed."
—NORA HOLLEY, *Bloomingdale's*

Feel the collar. If it's very stiff or lumpy, it means that the fusing inside the collar has been glued to the fabric, and it's not going to hold up well after laundering. And if the collar has tabs, they should be removable as washing tends to warp them and distort the collar shape.

"A good collar," says Nora Holley, "should last a year or even two or three before it begins to fray at the edges. If it doesn't last that long, however, it may not always be the shirt's fault—we've found that the whiskers of men with heavy beards tend to fray the collars of even the finest shirts very quickly.

"Most of the fabric used in dress shirts in this country comes from the same one or two mills in Japan. These mills produce different qualities of fabric, but generally the imported goods are superior to domestically woven ones. A well-made shirt can last anywhere from two to five years. The label on a good shirt will usually tell you if the fabric has been imported."

Better shirts have more attention paid to detail: A good shirt will always have a sleeve placket, preferably with buttons. A good button-down shirt will also have have a front placket, although that can be a matter of taste. Some men like shirts with French fronts, which have no placket—the fabric is just turned under and sewn near the buttons and buttonholes. The shirt with a front placket costs more, because it requires more fabric and installation work.

"A better shirt will have its label sewn to the collar. If it looks glued, it's been heat sealed and will pucker and peel after being washed and ironed a few times."
—STANLEY TUCKER,
Geoffrey Beene, Inc.

Single-needle tailoring, a process in which seams are sewn once, folded over, then sewn again for added durability and smoothness, is a desirable trait. Nearly all good dress shirts have single-needle collar and shoulder seams; very superior ones also have single needle sleeve and side seams.

As a general rule, you'll find that the best-made shirts don't skimp on fabric—and one of the places that generosity with fabric shows up is in the shirt's tail. A full, long tail practically guarantees that your shirt won't pull out of your trousers during the course of a day.

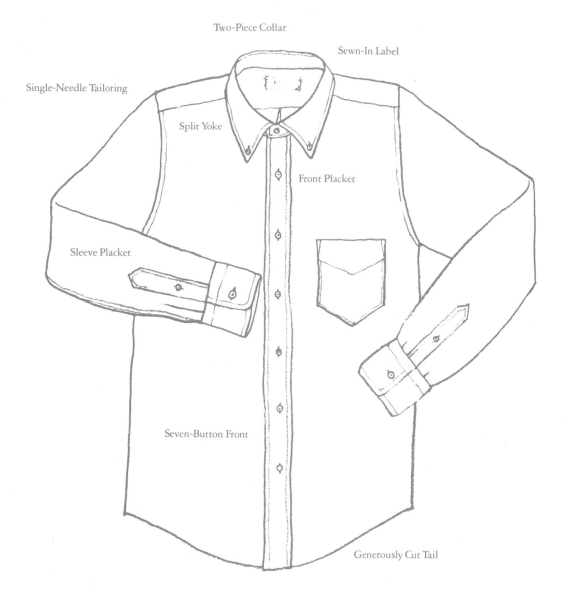

Two-Piece Collar

Sewn-In Label

Single-Needle Tailoring

Split Yoke

Front Placket

Sleeve Placket

Seven-Button Front

Generously Cut Tail

A WELL-FITTING SHIRT

Shirts are sized by the circumference of the collar and the length of the sleeve, measured from the nape of the neck to the base of the hand. Before you buy a shirt, make sure you know your exact measurements. Measure your neck, loosely, around the Adam's apple. (If, for example, you pull the tape measure snugly around your neck and it measures fifteen inches, you should buy a 15 1/2 shirt.) To measure arm length, begin at the center back of your neck, over the corner of your shoulder, then down to the elbow. Bend the elbow slightly and continue down to the wrist.

Many manufacturers now offer "average sleeve lengths," which means that instead of making a 33-inch sleeve and a 34-inch sleeve, they make one sleeve that is a 33-34. Manufacturers have to make, and retailers have to stock, fewer shirts this way, but they don't fit as well as the precisely sized shirts. If your arm is exactly thirty-four inches long, the 33-34 will be a bit too short and the cuff won't rest properly on your wrist.

When buying a dress shirt, you can choose from several styles. The *traditional fit* is fully cut and usually has a box pleat in the back that allows more freedom of movement. Although they're easy to move in, most traditional-fit shirts aren't baggy, like your grandfather's shirts were. They tend to be cut straight on the sides to eliminate bagginess. A traditional fit shirt will always be marketed in a fairly large package, and the package will say "traditional fit," give the shirt's measurements, or both.

"The pattern on the pocket should be aligned with the pattern on the body of the shirt."
—STANLEY TUCKER,
Geoffrey Beene, Inc.

A *fitted* shirt will be marketed in a slimmer package. Fitted shirts, modeled after closely cut European styles, have a fairly high armhole and tapered sides, giving a slimmer silhouette and less freedom of movement. The word "fitted" will normally be stamped on the package or in the shirt's collar. Not every man can wear fitted shirts, although every man can look good in the fuller traditional cut. "Even a very thin guy can wear a full-cut shirt," says Holley. "I think they're much more elegant than the fitted shirts."

In between these two styles fall the *regular fit* (sometimes called *designer fit*) shirts. Not as full as the traditional cut, the regular-fit shirt is fuller than the sharply tapered fitted shirt. "Anyone who normally wears a fitted shirt can definitely wear a regular fit shirt," says Holley, "and he'll find that he has a greater selection to choose from. And most men who wear the traditional fit, unless they're really very broad, can also wear the regular fit."

COLLAR STYLES

No matter what style collar you prefer, it should hug your neck gently, not press into your skin or gape away from it. The shape of your neck and face will determine how close to your face the top of the collar should be. (The height of the collar is usually called the slope.) High-slope collars look best on men with long faces and necks, while low-slope collars complement men with round faces and thick necks. There is also a medium-slope, which is fine for the man whose face is neither round nor thin.

The two most versatile collar shapes are the *standard* and the *button-down*. Both have a conservative three-inch point (the distance between the collar tip and the neckband) and a moderate spread (the distance between the collar tips), making them appropriate for wear with nearly any style suit. A four-in-hand tie knot looks best with the standard collar; the button-down, which takes its name from the two small buttons that fasten the collar tips to the front of the shirt, looks well with any knot.

Standard Collar with Four-in-Hand Knot

Button-Down Collar with Half-Windsor Knot

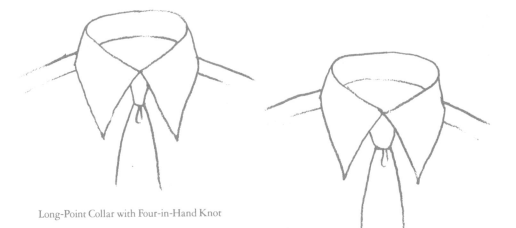

Long-Point Collar with Four-in-Hand Knot

Long-Point Collar with Half-Windsor Knot

The stylized *long-point* collar looks best with more dramatic clothing, such as closely cut European suits and shirts. Its points, which measure four to four and a half inches, can make large and round faces look narrower. It has a fairly small spread and looks best with a four-in-hand or half-Windsor knot.

French Collar with Windsor Knot

The *French* collar, which has short points and a wide spread, can help a very long, thin face look a little broader. It looks well with the large Windsor knot.

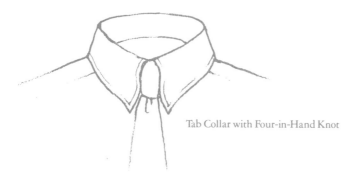

Tab Collar with Four-in-Hand Knot

A *tab* collar, which has removable stays that slip into the collar points and are removed prior to laundering, makes a shirt slightly more expensive because it costs more to manufacture the stays. The smooth, clean collar line the stay provides is worth the added expense.

Many dress shirts have a white collar, a sophisticated touch that emphasizes the color of the shirt, highlights the necktie, and flatters the face.

French Cuff

CUFFS

Most shirts feature cuffs that button, also called *barrel* cuffs. If this is the style you favor, look for cuffs that have two buttons, which allow for a more precise fit. If you want a dressier look, you can choose the double-folded *French* cuffs that are fastened with cuff links. "The barrel cuffs are classic," says Holley, "but French cuffs are becoming more fashionable. A lot of the better lines are doing French cuffs. I think they're very elegant."

Shirts worn with dinner jackets should be placed in individual laundry bags or wrapped in white tissue paper to keep them clean between wearings.

SHIRT FABRICS

Acetate, a silky looking fiber, is usually blended with cotton, rayon, or silk. It wrinkles easily and should be dry cleaned unless the care label says otherwise. Trade Names: Acele, Avicolor, Avisco, Celanese, Celaperm, Celara, Chromspun, Estron.

Acrylic, a strong, lightweight fiber, is available in a wide range of weights and textures. It holds creases and pleats well, and tends to resist wrinkling. Most acrylics can be machine-washed, and ironing is rarely necessary. Trade Names: Acrilan, Creslan, Courtelle, Orlon, Zefkrome, Zefran.

Batiste is an extremely lightweight, soft fabric that is usually woven from cotton but can also be made from linen, silk, or rayon.

Broadcloth, made from cotton or a cotton blend, has fine ribs running across its surface.

Challis, a delicate wool fabric, has a faintly ribbed texture.

Cotton, available in many weights and weaves, may be the ideal shirt fabric. It is strong, cool, comfortable, absorbent, and can be dyed to almost any color. It wrinkles easily and will probably shrink slightly when it is first laundered. Cotton should be washed in warm water to minimize shrinkage; adding a fabric softener will cut down on wrinkles. Most cotton shirts can be machine dried at a medium heat, but they'll have to be removed from the dryer

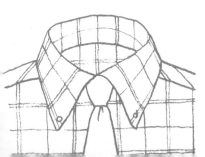

promptly or the wrinkles will set. Ironing while the shirt is still slightly damp will remove the wrinkles more easily.

Jersey, a soft knit fabric usually found in sport shirts, may be woven from cotton, wool, silk, acrylic, or rayon. It may be nearly sheer or very heavy.

Nylon, an extremely strong, elastic fiber, is easy to maintain and resists wrinkling. It does not breathe and tends to retain body heat. Nylon can usually be machine washed and dried. Trade Names: Antron, Blue C, Caprolan, Cedilla, Celanese, Enkalure, Monvelle, Qiana, Touch, Ultron.

Oxford cloth, a durable cotton fabric, has a soft and comfortable texture.

Piqué is a sturdy fabric woven from cotton or synthetic fibers. It sometimes has a faint pattern woven onto its surface.

Polyester, a durable and wrinkle resistant fiber, is available in a variety of weights and textures. It is often blended with natural fibers to give them its easy-care qualities. On its own, polyester tends to look unpleasantly shiny and to hold body heat. Most polyester can be machine washed in warm water and machine dried at a medium heat. Trade Names: Avlin, Blue C, Dacron, Encron, Fortrel, Kodel, Quintess, Trevira, Vycron.

READING LABELS

Every shirt will contain both a general brand or store label and a garment-care label that lists the fibers present in the shirt and gives instructions for its care. In a better shirt, these labels will be sewn in. A label that's glued or heat sealed will sometimes pucker when the heat sealing gives way, and will eventually come off.

IRONING

Most irons have a label that will tell you the proper temperature to use for different fabrics. If you're ironing a shirt that's a blend of several fibers, set the iron for the most delicate fiber present.

If you like your shirts crisply starched, spray starch is easy to use. Spray it on and let it soak into the shirt for a few seconds before you begin ironing so that the material has time to absorb it. Otherwise, mist the shirt so it's slightly damp before you begin.

1. Turn up the the collar of the unbuttoned shirt and lay it face up on an ironing board.

2. Start with the collar, ironing from its points to the center.

3. Iron around and behind the buttonholes and buttons.

4. Turn the shirt over to iron the back of the collar, the yoke, and the back of the shirt.

5. Fit the end of the ironing board into the shoulders to iron them.

6. Iron inside and outside the cuffs.

7. To iron the sleeves, run the iron along the underseams first and then iron from the tops of the sleeves down into the gathers at the cuff and back up toward the shoulder, where the crease is on most shirts. (If you prefer, you can choose the crease favored by the Prince of Wales and the Duke of Edinburgh—one that falls on the inside of the sleeve rather than at the top.)

FOLDING AND STORING SHIRTS

You can fold a shirt as well as the professionals do by following these steps.

EVERYDAY SHIRTS

1. Fasten the middle button and lay the shirt face down on a table or bed.

2. Fold one side in a third of the way toward the center of the shirt's back.

3. Fold the sleeve on the folded side over the back so it lies straight from the shoulder to the tail.

4. Repeat on the other side. (The second sleeve will lie partly over the first.)

5. Bring the tails up over the cuffs, then fold the shirt in half, so the bottom of the shirt reaches the base of the collar.

6. Lay the shirt face up in a drawer or on a shelf.

"I like a dress shirt with two buttons on the sleeve placket. The second button was first used in the days when no flesh was supposed to be visible, not an ankle or a bit of your arm. I think that extra button gives a much smoother line to the sleeve."
—NORA HOLLEY, *Bloomingdales*

Proper folding and storage will keep your shirts looking fresher longer. Avoid handling them unnecessarily—if you have the room, spread them out in drawers so that you can easily see the one you're looking for. If you have to conserve space, create a slightly angled stack of shirts so that you can see a bit of the side of each shirt in the stack. Rummaging through the drawers to find the shirt you need will only wrinkle all of them, so always remove all of the shirts that lie on top of the one you want—don't just yank one from the bottom.

EVENING SHIRTS

1. Spread two sheets of tissue out on a bed or table and lay the shirt face down across their width. The shirt must lie in the middle, with the collar touching one broad edge of the tissue. The bottom half of the shirt may extend beyond the opposite edge.

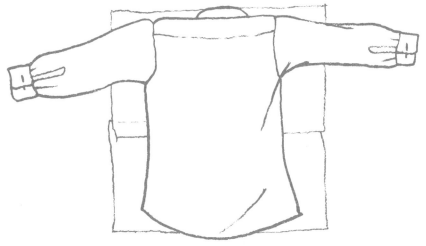

2. Fold it as you would an ordinary shirt, unless it has French cuffs that require cufflinks. If it does, the cuffs should lie at the top of the shirt near the collar so you can put the cufflinks in before you unfold the shirt. Step 3 shows how to do that.

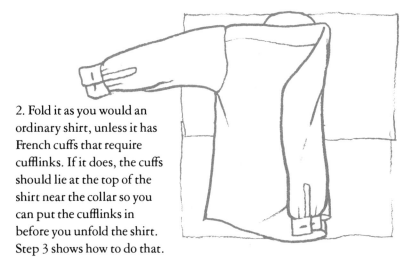

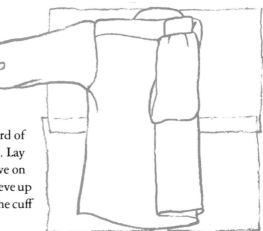

3. Fold one side in a third of the way across the back. Lay the corresponding sleeve on top of it and fold the sleeve up at the elbow, bringing the cuff up to the collar.

4. Repeat on the other side.

5. Fold the shirt crosswise, bringing the hem up to the edge of the collar.

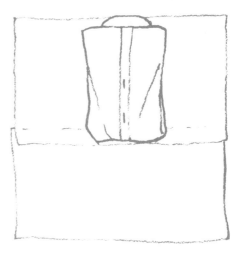

NECKTIES

A necktie is an integral aspect of your overall appearance. "A man's personality is reflected in his necktie," notes Geoffrey Beene. "There isn't that much flexibility in businesswear, except for the tie. He can express himself through the tie, and the one he chooses can change his whole look."

Don't select a necktie solely because of its color, pattern, or even fabric. You must first consider the tie's length, width, and construction.

DIMENSIONS

Most ties are between fifty-four and fifty-six inches long. A knotted tie should just brush the top of your belt line. (When buying a new tie, it's a good idea to bring an old one of the proper length along with you for comparison.) The width of ties varies with fashion, but don't just go along with the trends. Your tie should be balanced by the width of the lapels that you usually wear—narrower lapels call for a narrower tie, and vice versa. Shorter men should avoid very wide ties, as should heavy men. Tall, thin men can handle the broadening effect of a wide tie.

CONSTRUCTION

A well-made tie will have an interlining to help it keep its shape. The thinner the outer fabric, the thicker the interlining should be—you can tell by rubbing the tie gently between your fingers. Hold the tie straight out in front of you and see how it looks. If it pulls to the side slightly, the outer fabric has been stretched too tightly over the interlining, a fault that can't be corrected.

Check the back of the tie for the "bar tac"—a small horizontal stitch. There should be one at the broad end and another at the narrow end to keep the edges of the fabric from separating. Each should be a single, neat stitch, without any fabric pulling or puckering on either side of it.

FABRICS

The richest-looking (and most expensive) ties are made of silk. An elegant silk tie is easy to knot, looks luxurious, and is appropriate all year round. There are several kinds of silk used in ties, including shantung, which is made of irregular yarns and gives the tie an interesting rough texture; grenadine, a light silk with an irregular surface; and faille, a very soft silk with a faintly ribbed texture. If cost is a consideration, silk-and-polyester blends look very much like the real thing, for less money.

Excellent, crisp-looking ties are also fashioned from various weights of wool. Challis, a finely woven wool, makes particularly good lightweight ties; other wool ties tend to have a slightly coarser texture.

"People always give me knit ties as gifts, because they're practically all I wear. I like them because you can crumple them up and they won't wrinkle."
—GEOFFREY BEENE

Complement your lightweight summer suits with light, relatively inexpensive cotton ties.

COLORS AND PATTERNS

When buying solid ties, remember that clear, deep colors are always more appealing than bright, flashy ones. However, a complete tie wardrobe will consist of more than just solids. You'll want to include striped ties, a category that includes: *rep*, a diagonally striped tie named for the distinct diagonal weave of its fabric; *regimental stripes*, which originally carried the colors of a British man's old army regiment but is now essentially the same as a rep tie; *club* ties, which have a small repeating pattern (usually of heraldic devices or sporting symbols); and *ivy league* ties, which offer a small geometric pattern on a solid background. Very small polka dots and checked patterns are also correct, as long as they're subdued. Ties with many colors or large figures or patterns are strictly for very casual wear.

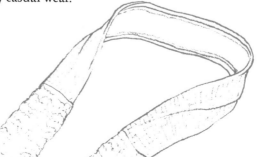

KNOTTING A TIE

There are, of course, three widely used, standard knot styles for your tie: The *four-in-hand*, the *half-Windsor*, and the *Windsor*. Each has its own characteristic look and contours. The knot you choose on any given day should be dictated by your physical size, the style of the shirt collar you're wearing, and the cut of your jacket.

In essence, these are a selection of knots that can be used to match and accent specific looks. It makes sense to master these simple techniques so you don't tie every necktie the same way with every look. For relatively heavy fabrics, such as knits and wools, and for small-spread collars, such as the tab, the four-in-hand is ideal. It uses less fabric than a Windsor or half-Windsor knot and so offers a sleeker look.

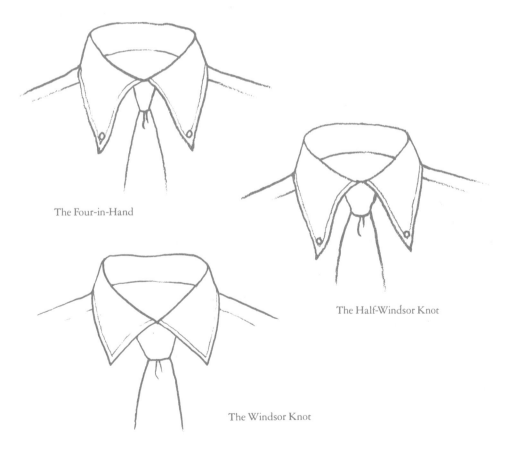

The Four-in-Hand

The Half-Windsor Knot

The Windsor Knot

The half-Windsor is the best choice for standard spread or buttoned-down shirt collars. When used with lightweight foulard silk ties it adds reasonable bulk to the look of the tie. The Windsor—the most stylized of the three basic knots—is best with wide-spread collar points. Because the knot is made up of one more twist than the half-Windsor and two more twists than a four-in-hand, you should buy ties at the longest end of the spectrum if you favor this look.

TYING A WINDSOR KNOT

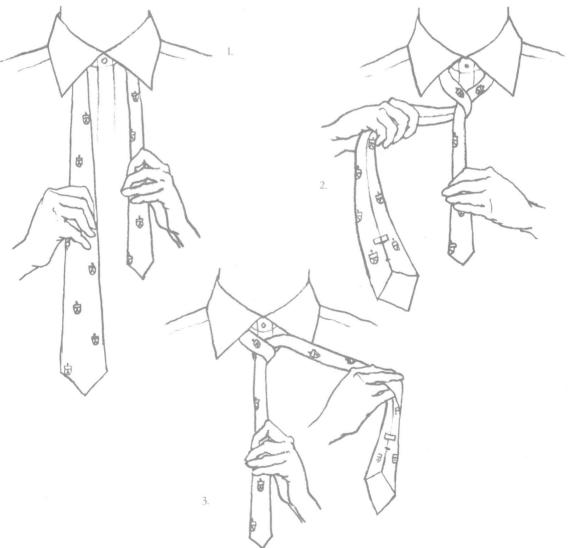

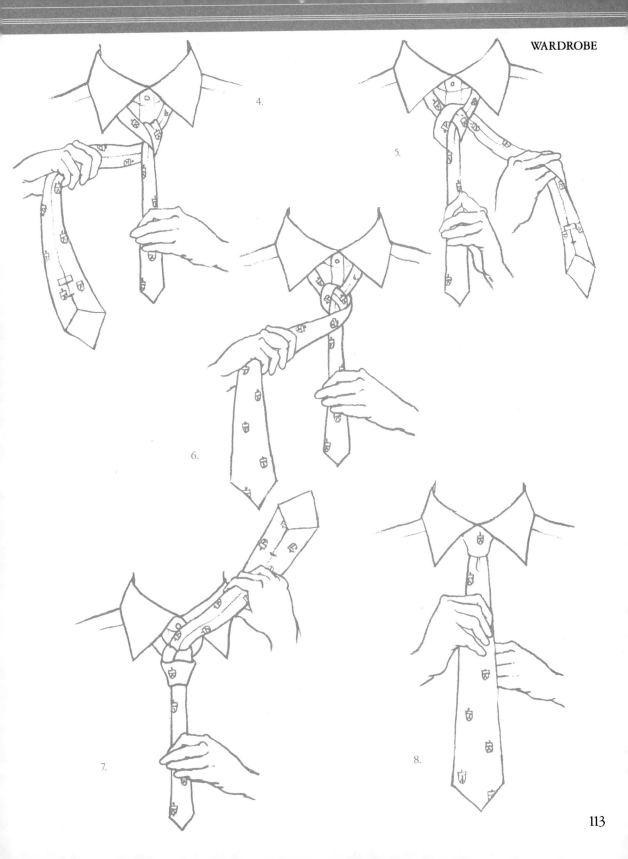

4.

5.

6.

7.

8.

TYING A HALF-WINDSOR KNOT

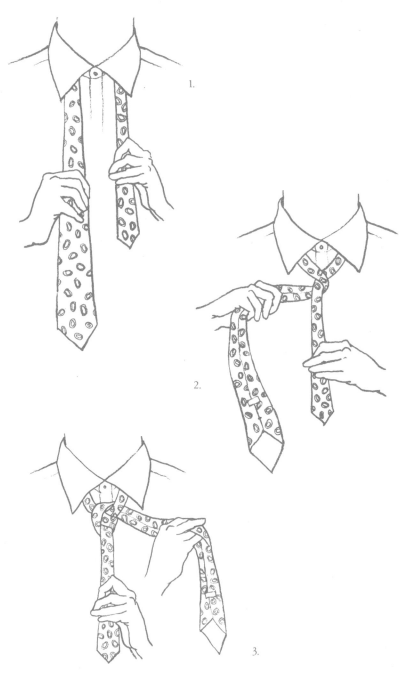

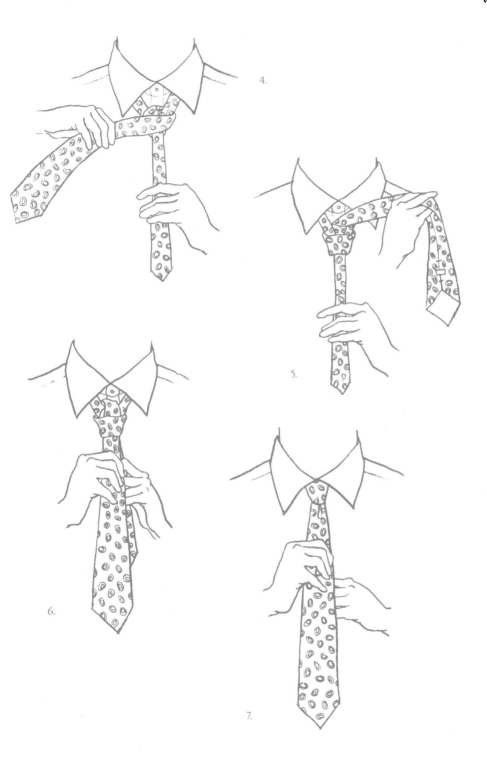

4.

5.

6.

7.

TYING A FOUR-IN-HAND KNOT

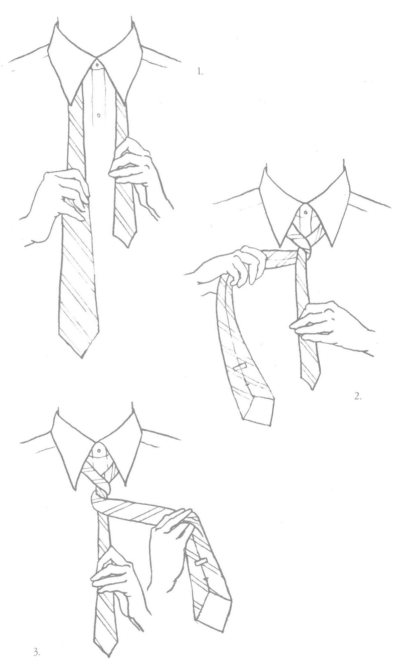

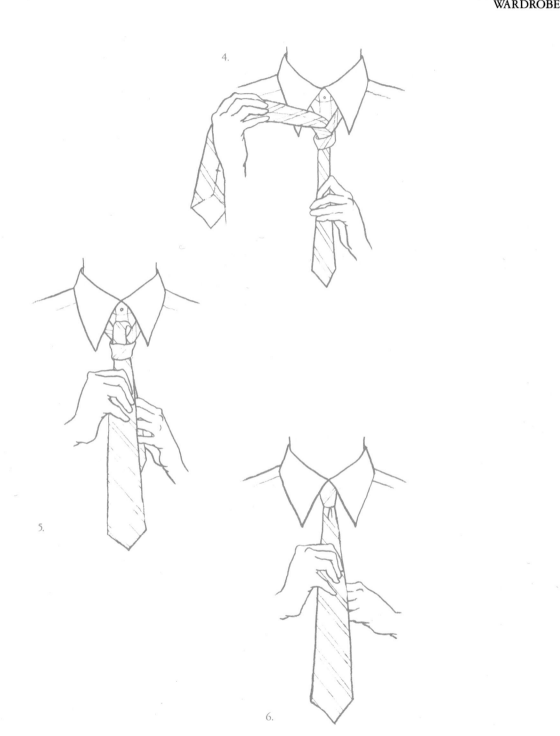

4.

5.

6.

TYING A BOW TIE

Bow ties are seen with increasing frequency as businesswear and are essential for formal occasions, but few men know how to tie one properly. Don't resort to the clip-on variety—they're not nearly as attractive as a proper bow tie.

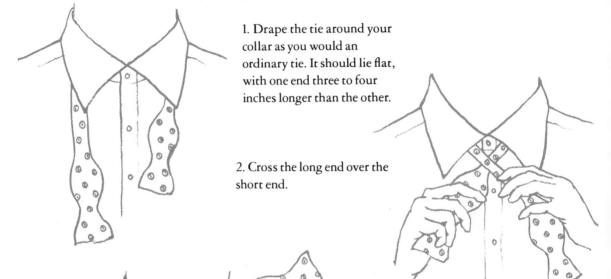

1. Drape the tie around your collar as you would an ordinary tie. It should lie flat, with one end three to four inches longer than the other.

2. Cross the long end over the short end.

3. Pass the long end behind the short end, creating a knot. The long end should be hanging over the shorter end.

4. Pull the tie tight around your neck. Fold the short end at the point where it flares to its bow width. Bring the folded portion up and hold it so that the fold points toward the long end and the narrowest point is in the center.

5. Bring the long end down over the center. The short end is now in a position to form one half of the bow, so hold it in place.

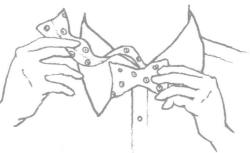

6. Fold the long end at the point where it flares to its bow width. Bring the folded long end up behind the folded short end and pass it between the short end and the knot.

7. The fold should emerge behind the single side of the short end, resulting in a loose knot.

8. The front and back bow are each composed of a single and a double end. Tighten the bow by taking hold of both double ends and pulling them tight.

9. Center the bow by gently pulling the two single ends. If this seems to have loosened the knot a bit, repeat steps 8 and 9 once or twice until the bow is properly centered and tightened.

STORING TIES

When you remove a tie, undo the knot gently and completely. Tugging at it will stretch the fabric, and leaving it partially knotted will put a permanent crimp in the fabric. Most ties should be hung over a tie rack or over the towel-draped crossbar of a hanger. Knitted ties, however, should always be folded as hanging can stretch them. Fold them in half, with the narrow end lying over the broad end. They can be folded in half again, if necessary.

HOW TO STEAM A TIE

You should never have to iron a tweed or knitted tie that's been stored properly, and silk ties should be steamed rather than pressed. Use a steamer, or stand an iron on its end and wrap a damp cloth around it.

1. Hold the tie in front of and slightly above the cloth-wrapped iron. Hold a clothes brush in the other hand.

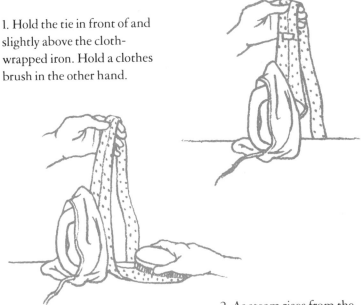

2. As steam rises from the iron, lower the tie gradually so that each part of it rests briefly on the cloth. Brush out the wrinkles as the tie slides over the cloth.

SWEATERS

A sweater can be one of the most versatile items in your wardrobe. Although sweaters are usually regarded as casual dress, a lightweight V-neck sweater (with or without sleeves) can be a stylish and colorful accent worn under a sport coat.

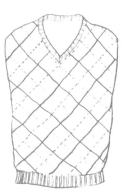

Your other sweater choices include: the *crew neck*, a round-necked sweater with ribbing on the cuffs and collar line; the *boat neck*, with a horizontal neck opening that runs from shoulder to shoulder; the *turtleneck*, with a high, narrow neck that folds down over itself; and the *cardigan*, which buttons down the front.

The best sweaters of any style are "fully fashioned," which means that they've been knitted as a whole rather than sewn together from separate pieces.

Sweaters are available in many different weights, also called gauges. The gauge is based on the size of the needle used to knit the sweater: the higher the gauge, the thinner the sweater. "A thirty-two gauge sweater would be almost a shirt weight," says Stanley Tucker. "You could wear it against your body. As the gauges get lower, the sweater gets bulkier—a three-gauge sweater would be a very bulky, outdoor sweater." Most sweaters at the moderate and upper moderate price level are about a seven gauge, which is thin enough to be worn under a suit jacket.

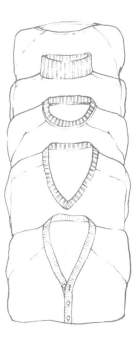

The yarn used in constructing the sweater also has an effect on its bulkiness. Many sweaters today are made of acrylic, which often resembles wool very closely. Acrylic, however, can never convincingly imitate cashmere, which can be made into very warm yet lightweight sweaters. A thin, two-ply cashmere sweater costs upward of $100; a heavy, two-ply cashmere sweater will probably cost $200 or more.

If you're shopping for a patterned sweater, hold it by the sides and pull gently. If it "grins"—the pattern separates to reveal the threads underneath—it's been cheaply made and won't wear well.

A WELL-FITTING SWEATER

Sweaters are sized by your chest measurement or as small, medium, large, and extra large. Although the fit depends a great deal on the style of the sweater, most sweaters, except heavy outdoor sweaters, should fit fairly close to the body. But not so close that they're uncomfortable—the best thing about sweaters is the fact that they're meant to let you move around unrestricted. Pay particular attention to the fit of the arms and shoulders—the shoulders of the sweater should hug your own fairly closely, but there shouldn't be any pulling around or under the arms.

Look for sweaters with cuffs and necklines that fit fairly closely, because these parts are sure to stretch with wear. To minimize this, never yank a sweater off roughly—removing a sweater with care will prolong its life.

SWEATER CARE

All sweaters should be aired after you've worn them to allow the fibers to freshen. (This is especially important if you've been in a smoke-filled room.) You can hang them in the open air for a few minutes before putting them away. When you store a sweater, however, it should be folded and laid down flat. Hanging a sweater for an extended length of time will stretch it out of shape.

WASHING A SWEATER

Most fine wool sweaters should be professionally dry-cleaned and blocked back into shape. Washable sweaters will last longest if you wash them by hand in cool water. Don't use harsh detergents on sweaters. Instead, use a wool wash product, such as Woolite, or ordinary hair shampoo, which will clean the garment without drying the fibers.

TO BRUSH A SWEATER

Sturdier sweaters, such as those made from shetland wools, acrylic, and lambswool should be brushed gently after each wearing. Don't brush very delicate fibers, such as angora or mohair—the bristles can tear them.

The brush you use on your sturdy sweaters should be softer than the one you use on heavy suitings—a child's hairbrush works well.

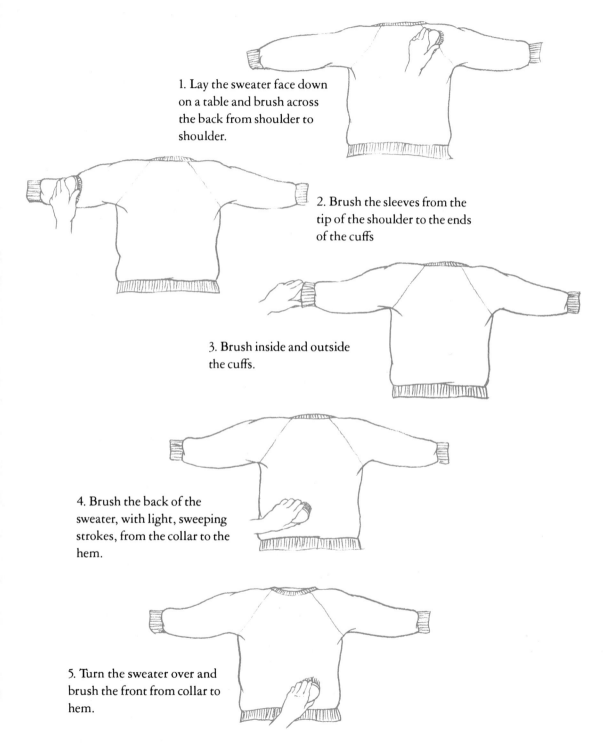

1. Lay the sweater face down on a table and brush across the back from shoulder to shoulder.

2. Brush the sleeves from the tip of the shoulder to the ends of the cuffs

3. Brush inside and outside the cuffs.

4. Brush the back of the sweater, with light, sweeping strokes, from the collar to the hem.

5. Turn the sweater over and brush the front from collar to hem.

BELTS

A belt is meant to be unobtrusive and functional, not a focal point of your outfit. It should be leather, about an inch wide, and have a handsome but simple buckle. There is simply no place for very wide belts or ornate buckles in the business world.

CHOOSING A BELT

A well-made belt has five holes and is sized from the buckle end to the middle hole, not the last hole. Always try a belt on with the trousers you plan to wear with it—the combination of a heavy shirt and trousers can add an inch or so to your normal waist measurement. Notice if the belt fits the belt loops on the trousers. If the belt is too wide for the loops, it will eventually tear them: If it's too narrow, it will slide up and down within them.

STORING BELTS

Curling belts up in the bottom of a drawer can warp and crack the leather. Instead, hang them by the buckle.

SOCKS

Socks are an invisible part of your look—unless they clash with your suit or fall down around your ankles. Always wear good over-the-calf hose in simple, solid black, navy blue, brown, or grey, depending on your outfit.

STORING SOCKS

You can roll socks up in a ball or fold them so that they are ready to slip over your feet.

1. Turn one sock inside-out.

2. Reach in the sock and pull the toe and heel up into it.

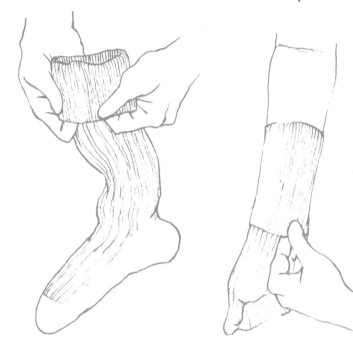

4. Keep the pair together by rolling the top of one sock down a couple of inches over the other.

3. Repeat with the other sock.

HANDKERCHIEFS

Not every man feels comfortable wearing a pocket handkerchief, but if you feel one would fit your style, it can be a striking accent to any suit. The twenty-inch-square of cotton, linen, or silk that you fold to create a fashion accessory can be of simple, crisp white, or a color or pattern that will accentuate a color in your tie. (One caution—don't wear a handkerchief in a pattern identical to your tie's pattern. It will look overdone.)

TO FOLD A HANDKERCHIEF

The *triangle* is especially good for plain handkerchiefs. Fold the fabric in half diagonally, then fold in the sides and bottom so the handkerchief sits in the pocket with just the point of the triangle showing.

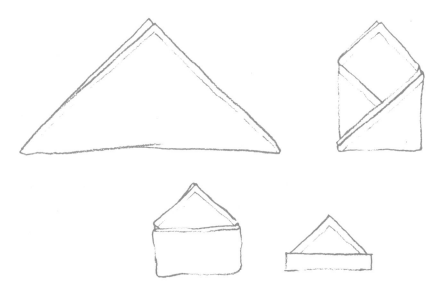

The *casual fold* is created by grasping the fabric at its center and tucking that center piece down into your pocket so that the handkerchief's corners peek up from the pocket in a casual, irregular manner.

The *puff*, another casual look, is created by grasping the fabric at its center and then, still holding the center, tucking the corners of the handkerchief down into your pocket. The puff will show above the pocket.

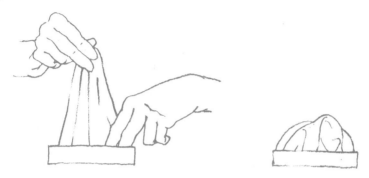

The *petal fold* works best with light fabric. Fold the handkerchief in half diagonally to form a triangle, then repeat once or twice to form more triangles. Tuck it into your pocket with the tips of the triangles showing.

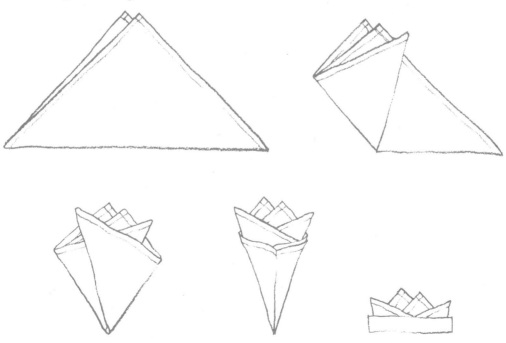

UNDERWEAR

Whatever underwear you're buying, always choose items made of cotton or other natural fibers. They're more comfortable, more absorbent, cooler to wear, and longer-lasting. White underwear made from polyester tends to turn yellow after it's been washed and bleached several times; cotton never will.

"Americans are very cruel when it comes to washing underwear," says Nan Puryear, the men's underwear buyer for Bloomingdale's in Manhattan. "They don't treat it carefully. Europeans will wash socks and underwear by hand; Americans are lazy about things like that. They throw things in the washer and dryer or send them out to a laundry that uses harsh detergents. This cuts down on the life of the underwear."

With such harsh treatment, you can expect good-quality underwear to last only an average of one hundred washings, or somewhere between one and two years.

BRIEFS AND BOXER SHORTS

Briefs, boxer shorts, and tapered boxer shorts are sized by waist measurement, or as small (28-30), medium (32-34), large (36-38), and extra-large (40). Like undershirts, they will shrink from 3 to 5 percent when first laundered, but manufacturers always allow for such shrinkage.

Although boxer shorts have traditionally offered a long, baggy fit and have been regarded by most men and women as the kind of outdated underwear their fathers wore, fashion has changed all that. The new tapered boxers (sometimes called fashion boxers), which originated in Europe, offer a much trimmer fit. Unlike traditional boxers, which tend to bunch up under tight or smooth-fitting trousers, tapered boxers can be worn under almost anything. They differ from regular boxers in that they don't have the full "balloon" seat, are cut two inches shorter, and usually have a slit on the side. They are available in a wide range of bright colors and prints and look more like running shorts than regular boxers.

"I've seen them in black and white and colors, with big dots, little dots, triangles, stripes—they're a lot more exciting than traditional boxers," says Nan Puryear. "The fashion boxers can cost anywhere between $12 and $35 a pair. A lot of men wear them because you can treat them almost like leisure wear. A man can go home after work and walk around the house in the shorts and still look good. You probably wouldn't do that with briefs."

"Briefs and boxers outsell undershirts by about four to one."
—NAN PURYEAR, *Bloomingdale's*

Briefs, which have fitted waist and leg bands, fit more closely than boxer shorts. In both boxers and briefs, the construction of the waistband is critical to the item's longevity. Avoid waistbands (and, in briefs, legbands) made with rubber, which will quickly dry and crack during machine washing and drying. Bands made of plain elastic aren't much better, although a woven elastic band knitted into the garment will hold up quite well. The very best bands are made of Lycra-spandex, a fabric containing 20 percent stretchable Lycra. A Lycra-spandex band is flexible enough to be comfortable yet strong enough not to stretch out with wear.

Some more costly briefs and boxers are made of cotton that has been "mercerized," a process that strengthens the cotton and makes it look and feel more like silk.

UNDERSHIRTS
Undershirts come in three styles—the crew-neck T-shirt, the V-neck T-shirt, and the sleeveless athletic shirt, which has a U-shaped neck.

"A lot of men don't feel dressed if they're not wearing an undershirt," says Puryear. "They like the fact that the undershirt will absorb perspiration before it shows through the shirt. White is really the only color that's acceptable for an undershirt that's being worn underneath clothing. Brighter colors will probably show through your shirt."

A T-shirt will usually shrink from 3 to 5 percent when it is first laundered, but the shirt's weave demands that it shrink only in length, not width. "The manufacturers make them that way because they can always cut them a little longer to allow for shrinkage and the shirt will still fit you," explains Puryear. "If the shirt shrinks a bit in width, it will stretch back to size the next time you wear it. It won't do that lengthways, so they have to make them long."

When buying an undershirt, look for one with a generously cut armhole. If it's not full enough to fall comfortably under your arm, the sleeve of the shirt will bind you. Next, check the rise of the neck. A very high-rise neck is crisp looking, but probably uncomfortable. The neck should be low enough to rest comfortably below the collar of your outer shirt. If you plan to wear the undershirt with an open-collar shirt, a V-neck or U-neck is a better choice than the higher-fitting crew neck. If you'll be wearing the T-shirt underneath a shirt of a light fabric, it's better to buy a sleeveless one since it won't create a sleeve line that will show through your shirt.

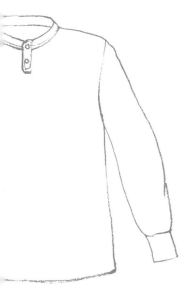

All undershirts are sized either according to your chest measurement or as small, medium, large, and extra large. Most good undershirts fit the body closely and can be worn under tapered shirts without wrinkling.

THERMAL UNDERWEAR
Essential for outdoor winter sports, thermal underwear can also be worn as loungewear at home by both men and women. The quality checks for thermal underwear are the same as for other underwear —look for all-cotton construction, generous armholes, and waistbands made of Lycra-spandex or woven elastic rather than rubber or plain elastic. Duofold makes an excellent line of thermal underwear.

UNDERWEAR AS OUTERWEAR
Because men's underwear is now being made in an array of colors and patterns, both men and women are adapting it for use as more than underwear. In fact, underwear can make surprisingly inexpensive and attractive streetwear.

"The colored T-shirts aren't meant to be worn under clothing," says Puryear. "They're good summer streetwear for both men and women. They look good with shorts. In cooler weather, they can be layered over or under other shirts—a black knit short-sleeved crew neck T-shirt looks terrific under a white U-necked athletic shirt. They're a very good buy, especially for women. In a ladies' department, similar T-shirts may cost $30 or more.

"We also sell patterned tapered boxer shorts to women," she says. "They slip them on over a swimsuit and wear them to the beach."

Thermal underwear can be adapted to other uses as well. Thermal tops, especially the kind that button at the neck, look especially well with jeans. And many women wear a man's thermal shirt instead of a nightgown in cold weather.

SHOES

Your shoes reflect the care you give them. Without proper care, shoes quickly grow scuffed, their heels run down, and their sides stretch out of shape. This damages more than just your appearance —if your shoes become very run down or misshapen, your body weight will settle into them incorrectly and you can develop back pains.

CHOOSING BOOTS AND SHOES

The skin and hides used vary with the type of boot or shoe you're buying, and the tanning process varies with different types of leather. As a general rule, look for leather linings, leather heels (which have thin bands of leather running around them), leather soles, and handstitching as signs of quality.

SHOE STYLES

Brogues, a popular lace-up style, are appropriate for business wear. Sometimes called the wingtip, the brogue is a sturdy, low-heeled shoe with a piece of perforated leather that resembles a bird's wings covering the toe.

The *oxford,* a lace-up shoe, offers exceptional versatility. You can choose a wingtip oxford, which is ideal for dark business suits but may be a bit too busy to wear with tweeds or very informal patterned jackets; the cap-toe oxford, which has a seam straight across the toe and is slightly more subdued and formal than the wingtip; or the very conservative plain-toe oxford, which, in black, is also appropriate for formal evening wear.

Loafers, like other slip-on shoes, used to be considered too casual for business wear, but that's no longer generally the case. Black penny loafers, tasseled loafers, or Gucci or Gucci-style loafers (with a distinctive gold or silver buckle on the front of the shoe) look well with suits or more casual trousers and jackets.

The *monk-strap* shoe, another slip-on, rests higher on the foot, making it resemble the sturdier lace-ups. It has a plain toe and fastens across the front of the foot with a buckle and strap.

WELL-FITTING SHOES

When you're planning to try on shoes, wear socks as thick as those you'll be wearing with the new shoes. How do the new shoes feel on your feet? Do they pinch? Are they too tight? Your little toe shouldn't be wedged up against the side of the shoe, and your big toe should be at least half an inch from the shoe's tip. You should be able to wiggle all your toes easily. Your heel should feel comfortably surrounded by the back of the shoe, not as though the edge of the shoe is cutting into it. Don't buy shoes that feel too snug and hope they'll loosen up a bit—odds are they won't. Avoid shoes with sharply pointed toes. They can throw off you off balance and cause leg and back pains. Square or softly rounded toes are a better choice.

Shoes that are too large are equally rough on your feet. Walk a few steps in the shoes—if your heels slip out as you walk, the shoes are too big and will rub against the back of your heels, causing blisters.

STORING SHOES

You'll save space, as well as wear and tear on your shoes, if you keep them on a shoe rack in the bottom of your closet. You can buy a rack at any department store, or make one from two curtain rods cut as long as your closet is wide. Just place them about an inch and a half apart, one above the other. Hook the heels of your shoes over the top rod and rest the soles against the bottom one.

Boots won't fit on a rack, so stuff them with trees or at least newspaper to keep them upright—never lay them on their sides.

POLISHING SHOES

Cream polish, which feeds fine leather and keeps it supple, or wax polish, which brings up a shine and is somewhat water resistant, will do the best job of shining your shoes. Meltonian Cream and Kiwi Wax Polish, available in a wide range of colors, are both excellent. Wax is best for sturdier shoes, while cream is better on delicate shoes. Before you polish any shoes, dust them thoroughly with a clean cloth. If you're using cream polish, you'll need a second clean cloth to apply the cream. If you plan to use wax, you'll need a small circular brush to apply the wax and a separate polishing brush.

Polishing brushes should always be kept dry, as water can make the bristles soft and useless. They have to be cleaned periodically to remove polish stuck between the bristles. To clean brushes, wrap two layers of brown paper, dull side out, over the edge of a table and rub the brush briskly against the paper.

When you polish, leave the trees in the shoes or put your free hand inside the shoe as far as you comfortably can. If the shoe has laces, remove them. Begin polishing at the toe, working back along the sides of the shoe.

For an extra-bright shine on sturdy leather shoes and boots, try the spit-and-polish technique outlined by Thomas Hill, who was an officer's servant in Britain's Coldstream Guards during World War II, and has been a valet and butler for over thirty years.

TO POLISH SHOES

1. Apply wax polish to one shoe with an applicator brush, and let it soak in while you apply a coat of polish to the other shoe.

2. Wrap the corner of a clean rag around your first and second fingers. Twist the rest of the rag into a coil to tighten the part around your fingers. Hold the end of the coil in the palm of your hand.

3. Dab the duster along the surface of the polish in the can.

4. Rub the polish into the toe with a circular motion. When the rag drags against the shoe, spit on the shoe as though spitting out an orange pip and rub the area again with the cloth. (Don't spit on the shoe if you've been eating sweets, which make your saliva too greasy. Instead, put a few drops of water in the upturned lid of the wax can and dip the rag briefly into that.)

5. Add more polish, a tiny bit at a time, to the rag and spit-and-polish each section of the shoe.

6. Lightly buff the polished shoe with the polishing brush. Don't scrub at it— you'll reduce the shine.

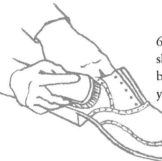

7. Finally, rub each shoe briskly with a chamois leather or a clean, soft cloth.

TO CLEAN SUEDE SHOES

1. Spray the outside of the shoes with a suede cleaner according to the instructions on the can.

2. When the cleaner has dried to a powder, brush it off with a wire brush. Use circular motions, from toe to heel, to bring up the nap.

COATS

A good coat represents an investment of anywhere between $400 and $1,000, so you'll want it to last for several years. An overcoat and a raincoat—or perhaps just a warmly lined trench coat—should be all the outerwear you need to buy.

A well-constructed coat will have the same features as a well-constructed jacket. It should be fully lined, the stitches should be small and unobtrusive (preferably done by hand), it should have generous seams, inside pockets, and cross-stitched buttons of bone or pearl, not plastic. Avoid "trendy" colors and styles. The classics—grey, navy, camel, and black—are your best bets when choosing a coat. They simply won't go out of style. Natural fibers are desirable in an overcoat, because they're unquestionably warmer than synthetics.

The very best overcoats are warm without weighing you down. "A good wool coat will be warm and very heavy," says Ralph DiNapoli, a buyer for Bloomingdale's in Manhattan, "while cashmere will provide warmth without the weight." Natural fibers must be treated carefully to ensure long life. "Dry-cleaning chemicals destroy the natural fibers," says DiNapoli. "I would clean a coat only once a season, if that. If it's not soiled and you don't think it needs to be cleaned, then don't do it. Brushing should keep it in good shape."

COAT STYLES

The *Chesterfield* coat, which may be single- or double- breasted, has a slightly fitted waist. The formal version of the Chesterfield, which has a black velvet collar, is perhaps the best-known example of this overcoat style.

The *British Warm* is modeled on coats worn by the British army during World War I. It has a slightly fitted waist, a flared bottom, epaulets, and angled pockets. It's not quite as classic a look as the chesterfield or balmacaan.

The *Balmacaan* offers a looser, more comfortable fit than the chesterfield. Its raglan sleeves (the seams of the sleeves run up to the neck of the coat rather than stopping at the shoulder) provide excellent shoulder and arm mobility. The balmacaan style is found in both overcoats and raincoats.

Chesterfield

British Warm

Balmacaan

Trench Coat

The *Trench* coat, practically a uniform for rainwear, also had its beginnings during World War I, as its name shows; British officers wore it in the trenches. Its detailing reveals its military background —the flap on the right shoulder cushioned the recoil of a rifle, the adjustable straps on the sleeves could be tightened against the weather, and the rings on the belt originally held canteens, grenades, or ammunition. Today's trench coats are made of tightly woven poplin or poplin blends, and many have zip-out linings that make them suitable for cold weather.

While trench coats and other rainwear are treated to make them water-repellent or water-resistant, water will still penetrate them if you stand out in the rain long enough. A non-porous rubber or vinyl coat is waterproof, but these fabrics can't breathe, unlike the water-resistant types, and soon become extremely hot and uncomfortable.

A WELL-FITTING COAT

When shopping for any kind of coat, wear the bulkiest suit you own to make sure the coat will fit comfortably over everything in your wardrobe. Look along the coat's back for vertical wrinkles, which indicate that it's too big, or horizontal wrinkles, which mean that it's too loose. The sleeves should extend about half an inch beyond your shirt cuffs. Length is important, both for style and protection; ideally, the coat's hem should hang below your knees. If the coat is belted, the belt should be at about the same level as the waistband of your trousers. If it's too high or low, the tailor can raise or lower the belt loops.

HANGING A COAT

Make sure you use a sturdy hanger with rounded ends that won't extend into the coat's sleeve. Don't hang it from the loop on the inside of the collar—the coat won't balance properly and can pull out of shape. Hang the coat as you would a jacket, with the shoulders evenly balanced and the center of the collar against the crook of the hanger.

TO BRUSH A COAT

Because a coat is bigger and bulkier than a jacket, the brushing technique is slightly different.

1. Empty the pockets and unfasten the buttons.

2. Hold the coat in one hand with the lining facing you. Use your free hand to brush the inside of the collar, then turn the collar over and brush the outside.

3. Hang the coat from a door frame with its back facing you.

4. Brush from the collar out to the edge of each shoulder.

5. Hold one sleeve taut and brush its back from cuff to shoulder, then back down again.

6. Repeat step 5 on the back of the other sleeve.

7. Hold the hem taut with one hand and brush up from the hem to the collar, then down again.

8. Turn the coat so that the front is facing you.

9. Brush the front of the sleeves the same way that you brushed the back, then brush inside and outside the cuffs.

10. Turn the collar and lapels up and brush underneath them.

11. Hold the hem taut with one hand and brush up from the hem to the collar, then down again.

12. Finish off by brushing between the buttons and turning the collar and lapels back down to give them a final brushing.

TO HELP WITH A COAT

It's easy to feel awkward when you're helping someone into her coat. To do it smoothly, hold the coat at the midpoint of each shoulder, making sure it's open enough for the person to slip into easily. Lift the shoulders slightly as she puts her arms through the sleeves. When her arms are through and the coat is resting on her shoulders, lift the coat again slightly to allow it to settle over her clothes properly.

HATS

Although many men don't bother with them, a hat can add a distinctive look to any outfit. There are many styles to choose from, and you should try several types to determine which ones best suit your face and hair.

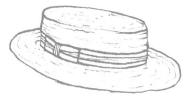

Boater or *Sennit*: A round, flat-topped straw hat popularized by vaudevillians. The boater is appropriate only for very casual summer wear.

Cloth: Strictly for casual wear, this is a fabric (usually wool) version of the Irish tweed hat, which has a high crown and a round, narrow brim. It is available in solids and tweeds.

Homburg: Designed for evening wear, the homburg has a tapered crown and a brim that curls on the sides.

Panama: The classic lightweight summer hat.

Planter's Hat: Modeled on hats worn by plantation owners in the tropics, this flat-topped hat has a curl on the edge of its brim and usually has a brightly colored band running around its crown. It is made of coconut palm or other light material.

Snap-brim or *Trilby*: A plain felt hat with a two-inch wide band of fabric running around the base of its crown, which usually has a crease down its center. The brim is turned down in the front and up in the back. The snap brim is appropriate for everyday wear.

Tyrolean: Modeled on the hats traditionally worn by Alpine yo-delers, this is a snap-brim style with two or more cords twisted around the base of its spine and a small brush stuck in the cords as decoration. It may be made from felt, wool, suede, or velour.

STORING HATS

Stack hats one inside the other, lining the inside of each with tissue paper before stacking to keep them clean.

TO BRUSH A HAT

It's best to brush felt hats near a steaming kettle, to help bring up the nap as you work.

1. Place your hand inside the hat's crown, with your fingers spread and your palm turned up. Press your thumb against the headband to balance the hat.

2. Beginning above the ribbon, brush in a clockwise direction, working toward the top of the hat. As you brush, turn the hat by rotating the hand inside the hat counterclockwise.

3. Brush around the brim.

STAIN REMOVAL

No matter how careful you are, the occasional stain is inevitable. You can save your clothes from being permanently marked, however, by knowing how to handle stains when they happen.

Caution is the key to successful stain removal. The chart beginning on page 146 offers sound general advice on removing common stains, but you have to use your judgement as well. When a delicate fabric or dry-clean-only garment is stained badly, you would probably do well to consult a dry cleaner. (The longer you let a stained garment sit your closet, the less chance there is of removing the stain. Fresh stains are easiest to remove.)

DRY CLEANERS

It's worth shopping around a bit to find a dry cleaner whose work pleases you. Look for one that does its work on premises, which reduces the possibility of your clothing being sent to a central plant and misplaced. Before taking a garment to the dry cleaner, completely empty its pockets and brush large pieces of lint from its surface. Suits should be folded carefully when being carried to the cleaners; rolling them up can damage the interlining.

Make sure you point out stains to the dry cleaner, telling him what the stain is and what, if anything, you've done to try to remove it.

HOME STAIN REMOVAL

Stains on washable fabrics—and some stains on non-washable fabrics—can almost always be successfully treated at home. The chart that follows offers guidelines, using the following terms:

Bleach solution: A 50-50 blend of bleach and water.

Dry cleaning solvents/Grease solvents: Commercially available spot removing substances.

Detergent solution: One teaspoon of liquid detergent (a dishwashing liquid will do) in one cup of warm water, or half teaspoon of powdered laundry detergent in one cup of warm water.

Enzyme solution: One tablespoon of a commercial pre-soak product (with the word "enzyme" on its label) mixed with a quart of water. This is especially good for lifting protein-based stains such as blood or egg yolk.

STAIN REMOVAL CHART

STAIN	WASHABLE FABRIC	NONWASHABLE FABRIC
BEER	Dab fresh stains with water; soak set stains in an enzyme solution for 30 minutes, then launder.	Sponge lightly with vinegar; rinse.
BLOOD	Soak fabric in cold water, changing the water in the basin to keep it clear. Sponge remaining traces with a detergent solution.	Sponge with a cold water and salt solution; blot dry.
BUTTER (or margarine)	Sponge with cold water, rub a bit of liquid detergent into the stain; rinse well with warm water.	Sponge with a dry-cleaning solvent.
CATSUP	Blot with paper towels, rinse with cold water, and rub a bit of liquid detergent into the stain.	Sponge with a dry-cleaning solvent and allow to dry. Repeat if necessary.

STAIN	WASHABLE	NONWASHABLE
CHOCOLATE	Soak in an enzyme solution for 30 minutes; launder as usual. If traces remain, sponge with a 50-50 solution of hydrogen peroxide and water.	Sponge with cool water, followed by a dry-cleaning solvent.
COFFEE (with milk)	Soak in an enzyme solution for 30 minutes, then sponge any remaining traces with a liquid detergent; launder as usual.	Blot the liquid with a paper towel, then sponge with a grease solvent. Let dry, repeat if necessary.
COFFEE (without milk)	Rinse with cool water, sponge with a liquid detergent, and rinse with warm water.	Place a towel under the garment and pour a small amount of water through the stain. If traces remain, sponge lightly with a solution of one teaspoon liquid detergent to one cup of cool water.
CREAM	Sponge with cool water and work a few drops of liquid detergent into the stain. Without rinsing, launder as usual.	Sponge lightly with cool water, then with a grease solvent, then again with cool water. Repeat as necessary.
FRUIT (and fruit juices)	Sponge with cool water, then dab lightly with white vinegar to keep the stain from setting. Soak in an enzyme solution and launder as usual.	Sponge with cool water and dab lightly with white vinegar. Take garment to the dry cleaners.

STAIN	WASHABLE	NONWASHABLE
EGG	Turn the garment inside-out and place it on a towel. Sponge cold water through the stain, soak the garment in a detergent solution, and launder in cool water. (Never use warm or hot water while treating an egg stain—the heat will cause the stain to set.)	Sponge lightly with cold water and let dry. Then sponge in a dry cleaning solvent and let dry.
GRAVY	Blot with paper towels, then soak in cold water. Sponge with a detergent solution and launder as usual.	Sponge with dry cleaning solvent.
GREASE	Rub a few drops of liquid detergent into the stain, rinse with water as hot as is safe for the fabric, and launder as usual.	Blot the stain and sponge lightly with a grease solvent.
GRASS	Rub liquid detergent into the stain, then sponge with detergent solution; rinse well.	Sponge lightly with rubbing alcohol, first testing the alcohol on an inconspicuous part of the garment to make sure it won't fade or discolor the fabric. If it does, have the item dry cleaned.

STAIN	WASHABLE	NONWASHABLE
LIPSTICK	Sponge stain with liquid detergent and rinse with warm water. Repeat as necessary, then launder as usual.	Sponge with a cleaning solvent; repeat as necessary.
MAYONNAISE	Place the stain over a towel, sponge it with cool water, and work in a few drops of liquid detergent. Launder as usual.	Place the stain over a towel, sponge it lightly, with cool water, and apply a grease solvent. Repeat as necessary.
MILDEW	Launder, using bleach if the fabric permits. Hang the garment to dry in the sun. If traces remain, sponge them lightly with lemon juice and salt or vinegar, and launder again. (Light or fresh mildew stains can be removed fairly easily; heavy or set stains may have damaged the fibers and are impossible to eliminate.)	Have the garment dry cleaned.
MUD	Allow the mud to dry, then brush the residue away. Sponge the remaining traces with cool water, work in a few drops of liquid detergent, and rinse with warm water.	Allow the mud to dry, then brush the residue away. Lightly sponge in a detergent solution, then rinse with warm water.

STAIN	WASHABLE	NONWASHABLE
NEWSPRINT	Sponge the stain with detergent solution, rinse with cold water, and launder as usual.	Sponge with detergent solution, then rinse by sponging with cold water.
OIL	Rub a few drops of liquid detergent into the stain, rinse with water as hot as is safe for the fabric, and launder as usual.	Blot the stain and sponge lightly with a grease solvent.
PEN (ballpoint ink)	Rinse stain with cold, running water, sponge with a detergent solution, blotting often with paper towels to keep from spreading the stain. Sponge with a dry-cleaning solvent and let dry. If the fabric can tolerate bleach, traces may be removed with a bleach solution.	Dab with dry cleaning solvent. If traces of the stain remain, have the garment dry cleaned.
PENCIL	Rub lightly with an eraser. If traces remain, rub a few drops of liquid detergent into the stain and rinse with warm water.	Rub lightly with an eraser. If traces remain, take the garment to the dry cleaner.
PERSPIRATION	Soak in an enzyme solution and launder as usual.	Have the item dry cleaned.

STAIN	WASHABLE	NONWASHABLE
SHOE POLISH	Scrape off as much as you can with the edge of a dull knife. Sponge stain with liquid detergent and rinse with warm water. Repeat as necessary, then launder as usual.	Scrape off as much as you can with the edge of a dull knife. Sponge with a cleaning solvent; repeat as necessary.
SOFT DRINKS	Sponge with cool water, followed by a detergent solution. Launder as usual.	Sponge lightly with vinegar and rinse with cool water.
TEA (with milk)	Soak in an enzyme solution for 30 minutes, then sponge any remaining traces with a liquid detergent; launder as usual.	Blot the liquid with a paper towel, then sponge with a grease solvent. Let dry, repeat if necessary.
TEA (without milk)	Rinse with cool water, sponge with a liquid detergent, and rinse with warm water.	Place a towel under the garment and pour a small amount of water through the stain. If traces remain, sponge lightly with a solution of one teaspoon liquid detergent to one cup of cool water.
WAX (floor, furniture)	Soak in an enzyme solution for 30 minutes, then sponge any remaining traces with a liquid detergent; launder as usual.	Blot the liquid with a paper towel, then sponge with a grease solvent. Let dry, repeat if necessary.

STAIN	WASHABLE	NONWASHABLE
WAX (candle)	Place garment in freezer to harden stain, or use a dull knife to remove as much wax as possible. Place the garment between two paper towels and press with a warm iron, changing the towels as they absorb the wax. Remove traces by sponging with a dry cleaning agent.	Try the method given for washable fabrics. (If the garment is especially delicate, take it to a dry cleaner instead.)
WHISKIES	Sponge with cool water, followed by a detergent solution. Launder as usual.	Sponge lightly with vinegar and rinse with cool water.
WINE (red)	Blot the stain with a paper towel, then sponge it with a warm detergent solution, followed by a rinse in cold, running water.	Blot the stain thoroughly, then mist it lightly with club soda. If stain remains, take it to a dry cleaner.
WINE (white)	Sponge the stain with cool water. If traces remain, apply a warm detergent solution and launder as usual.	Sponge the stain gently with club soda. If traces remain, take it to a dry cleaner.

THE TRAVELER

If Rudyard Kipling were alive and well and writing a travel column, you might well be reading:

"If you can board flights on schedule and delayed—and treat those two realities just the same/ If you can fly stand-by and keep your virtue—or fly first class and not lose the common touch / If you can keep your head while those that are milling about the luggage carousel are losing theirs,/ Then you'll be a Traveler, my son."

There's no question that travel is broadening, is increasingly necessary for many businesses, and is, at least in theory, available to more people. Whether you're logging miles on an Interstate highway, riding through the night on an Amtrak express train, or moving from a breakfast meeting in Chicago to a luncheon in Dallas in the reclining seat of a 747, travel is physically demanding. And, if you don't attend to details, it can also be emotionally difficult.

There is a marked difference between a Traveler and someone who is traveling. It's made up of small insights and personalized systems and a realization that the process of getting from where you are to where you want to be can carried out, at least to a degree, on your own terms.

Any traveling, for business or pleasure, causes a disruption in your daily routine. According to Leslie Grunberg, the president of Jacqueline Cochran Incorporated, who travels up to 150,000 miles a year, "Traveling, for people who travel a lot, is somewhat like a loss of identity. You lose where you belong. You lose sight of the people who know you. You lose your sense of belonging, as well as your sense of being unique. In hotels, you're just another traveler."

You can adjust more quickly to strange surroundings by approaching the experience thoughtfully. People who travel frequently on business develop their own techniques for dealing with travel. While there is no one "correct" method, consider the various approaches and decide which one most closely fits your own needs and lifestyle.

"When I travel," says Grunberg, "I concentrate on retaining my sense of identity. I do that by always staying in the same hotels in the cities I visit frequently, and by joining the various airline clubs. That way, when I'm at a hotel or in a plane, I'm likely to be greeted by name. It sounds like a small thing, but because I travel so much, it becomes psychologically very important. It keeps me from being just another body in seat 14A."

Grunberg minimizes the disruptive effects of business travel by condensing a trip into as little time as possible. "I try to do as many things in one day, or thirty-six hours, as I possibly can, and then fly back. I hate to dwell and stay over for more time than is necessary to do my job. I once went to Tokyo from New York for only twenty-four hours. It was a weird kind of experience, but I've found that I can do in twenty-four hours what other people do in three or four days. Instead of sleeping, I hold as many meetings as I can in twenty-four hours, and fly back. I find that's the only way to minimize distractions and keep the momentum of business going. The jet lag doesn't catch up with me until I return home where I'm better prepared to deal with it."

Executive recruiter James Hunt of Kinney, Kindler and Hunt has a travel schedule that demands minutely detailed planning—particularly on those occasions when he visits as many as four cities in a twenty-four-hour period. "I once arrived in New Orleans at night, had a 7 o'clock breakfast meeting the next morning, took a plane to Dallas for a meeting in Dallas airport, took a plane to Phoenix for a meeting in Phoenix airport, flew to Los Angeles merely to change planes, then flew on to San Francisco," he recalls. "To deal with the confusion that can sometimes accompany trips like that one, I always dictate my impressions of each meeting into a small tape recorder while I'm on the plane or waiting in the lounge. Style and grammar don't count then—it's just important to record all of your impressions before you forget. You can sort them out later."

Comfort and convenience are an an important part of dealing with travel, too. Most knowledgeable travelers, especially business travelers, avoid checking their luggage whenever they can—waiting for luggage to arrive after the plane lands simply wastes too much time, and there's always the possibility that the bags may be lost or damaged. The clothes a man normally needs to carry for the average business trip of a week or less—an extra suit, shirts, socks, underwear, ties, and perhaps spare trousers, a sport jacket, and a sweater—should fit in the soft–sided grip and garment bag that you're permitted to carry on the plane. Don't overpack—most hotels have good, efficient laundry facilities available should you find yourself running out of clean shirts in the middle of your trip. Once you've eliminated the need to check and reclaim your luggage, you can concentrate on the other details involved in making your flight as smooth and trouble-free is possible.

"For my part, I travel not to go anywhere, but to go. I travel for travel's sake. The great affair is to move."
—ROBERT LOUIS STEVENSON

If your trip is going to be a long one, or you're going on a vacation that requires a lot of clothes, you may not be able to avoid checking your luggage altogether. In that case, make sure you take a carry-on bag that contains the essentials—toiletries, a spare shirt or two, and a change of socks and underwear—just in case your luggage goes astray.

TRAVEL AGENTS

If you're a business traveler, your company probably takes care of travel arrangements for you, but if you're on your own a travel agent can make your trip smoother, and possibly even save you money. The maze of airfares, package deals, and tour options is maddening to the novice traveler, but a good agent can get you through it all. safely. A good agent will ask you questions about your likes and dislikes—are you looking for night life and bright lights? a quiet beach? great shopping? a luxury hotel? a rustic inn? sports facilities? sightseeing?—and try to formulate a trip based on your answers.

Unless you need very special arrangements, you don't pay a travel agent. He works on commissions paid by the airlines and hotels that can range from 7 to 20 percent of his bookings. This fact may tempt an unscrupulous agent to try to get you to spend more to increase his commission, but a good agent is more interested in giving you a good deal so that you'll use his services again. If you run into an agent who ignores your needs, leave his office and look for another agent.

In addition to understanding traveling rules and terminology better than you probably ever will, a good agent simply makes your life easier by doing all the telephoning for you. And he may well carry more clout than you do—a hotel that has no room when you call may find it when an agent who gives them business calls.

To find an agent, ask friends and business colleagues. If you're hunting for an agent on your own, remember that the biggest agencies, such as American Express and Thomas Cook, though they certainly do a good job, are probably no more efficient or effective than a well-established private agency. And the private agency is probably in a better position to give you personalized service. Look for an agency that's been around for a while, indicating that it has developed a circle of satisfied customers. And always look for the emblem of the American Society of Travel Agents (ASTA). It's no guarantee that the agency is good, but the society does have a code of ethics and a Consumer Affairs Committee for complaints.

PLANNING A FLIGHT

When you (or your travel agent) are booking a flight, be specific. If you can't bear smoke, request a seat that's well within the no-smoking section—there are no walls between sections, so you want to be a good distance away from the smokers. If you want leg room, aisle seats near the emergency doors are best. If a smooth ride is important to you, get a seat over the wings (rear seats tend to give the bumpiest ride).

Always book a return flight, even if you think your plans might change. It's better to try to change it later than to be stuck without one. And don't forget to confirm your seat reservation two days before your departure.

Before you leave for the airports, telephone ahead to make sure that everything's running on or near to schedule. There's no point in hurrying to make a plane that's not going to arrive at the airport for six hours.

IN TRANSIT

A trip really begins the minute you leave your home or office for the airport. Experienced travelers agree that racing through the terminal to catch a plane at the last possible minute is a bad way to begin. You want to reduce the tension present in an already stressful situation rather than add to it.

And whether you're traveling for business or pleasure, it's now more important than ever before to arrive at the airport with time to spare. Because of the federal deregulation that took effect in 1985, you're no longer guaranteed a seat on a crowded plane. Flights are often overbooked, and if you don't arrive at least thirty minutes before takeoff, you may find that your seat's been given to someone else. And there's virtually nothing you can do about it.

"I give myself a lot of time," says Leslie Grunberg. "I'll arrive at the airport early and make calls from the first-class lounge or the airline club lounge rather than being stressed. I prefer to arrive about fifteen minutes before due time, which is normally forty-five minutes before takeoff.

"I never travel without my diary. One should always have something sensational to read in the train."
—OSCAR WILDE

"I always reserve a taxi or limousine in advance. I never try to catch a cab at the last minute, in any city. I want the travel to be as smooth as possible. I like to step into a taxi, arrive at the airport, and calmly board the plane. The sequence should flow. And anything that disrupts that flow becomes an aggravation. Normal traveling fatigue and jet lag are enough of a problem, so I try never to add to them."

Henry Lambert, president of real estate development for the Reliance Group, flies coast to coast an average of once a week and agrees that arriving at the airport is a critical part of a flight, one that deserves some planning. "Although I don't normally like to use limousines," he notes, "booking a limousine or a radio taxi the day before the flight is really the most practical way of insuring that you'll arrive in plenty of time for your flight. Personally, I prefer just to hail a cab on the street, but I've come dangerously close to missing flights that way. I find that limousines are most likely to pick you up as scheduled, and they really don't cost very much more than taxis."

For those rare occasions when he doesn't arrive at the airport with time to spare, Lambert manages to save precious seconds by entering the terminal through the arrivals rather than the departures gate.

"There's usually a long line of traffic waiting to unload luggage outside the departures gate," Lambert explains, "and instead of pulling into that line, I go in the arrivals entrance. In most major airports, the arrivals section is directly below the departures area, and you need only walk up the stairs to check in. That trick has saved me many times."

James Hunt saves time at the airport by getting boarding passes from a travel agent. "Travel agents can give you boarding passes for a lot of airlines now, and it's very convenient. When I have several stops to make on a trip, I carry a pack of tickets and boarding passes for every flight. I don't have to stop anywhere, just go directly to the gate.

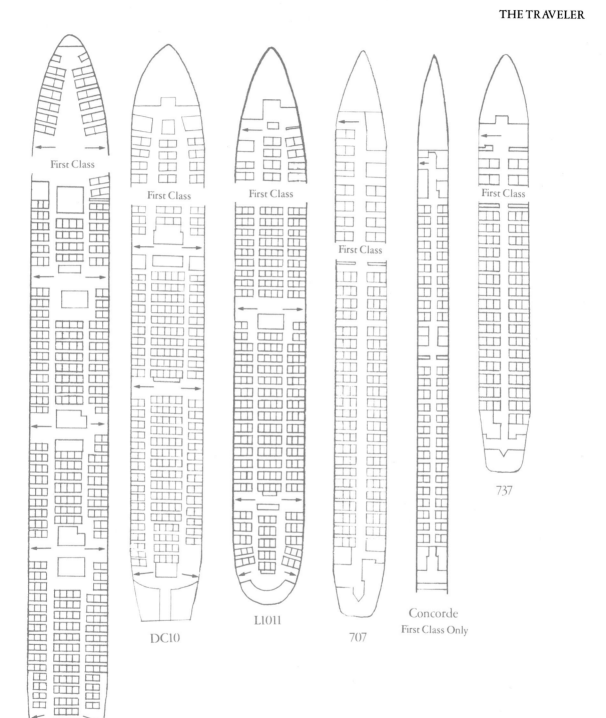

First Class

First Class

First Class

First Class

First Class

DC10

L1011

707

Concorde
First Class Only

737

747

Airline Passenger Seating

"I like to be one of the first people on the plane," he continues. "That way, there's plenty of room in the overhead compartments to stow my carry-on bags, and I don't have to try to stuff things under the seat. It means sitting there while everyone else walks down the aisle and bangs you on the head, but in the long run it's much more comfortable and convenient."

TRAVELING IN COMFORT

Because of the grueling travel schedule he maintains, Leslie Grunberg pays particular attention to his physical health. "I don't drink," he says, "and that makes a huge difference. I see business travelers on planes at 10 o'clock in the morning with dry martinis, and I don't understand it. They're obviously not going to be in any condition to work when they arrive. I drink water instead, and I use the time on the plane to work or read. Some travelers say 'I'm going to take one day off to reduce the jet lag when I arrive, and I'm going to take one day off when I get back.' I never do that.

"In addition to not drinking, I'm very careful to eat lightly, both on the plane and in a strange city. I try to avoid airplane food, because it's filled with preservatives. The only things I eat on planes are smoked salmon and caviar, because they aren't tampered with. I never experiment with food on a trip," he adds. "I always eat the same things—grilled fish, grilled meat, salad, cheese, yogurt. That's it. I do make one exception, though. Japanese food. Japan is the only place in the world where I will sample new restaurants.

"I'm also particular about where I sit on an airplane," he says. "I like the last seat on the aisle, because I have a touch of claustrophobia. That seat gives me more freedom to move, and that section tends to be less crowded. Once I know that type of plane I'll be on, I know the seat number to ask for."

Grunberg likes to bring his entertainment with him when he's traveling. "I love jazz," he says, "and I would never travel without my music. I carry a small Walkman with two big loudspeakers, and I will bring the music of one musician with me on a trip. I might bring six tapes by John Coltrane, or eight tapes by Thelonious Monk."

Henry Lambert pays particular attention to the comfort features and food offered by different airlines. "I go first class," says Lambert. "I often take night flights, so I prefer airlines that offer deep reclining seats, which make sleeping easier. An aisle seat is best, since you don't feel so boxed in, but I avoid the last or next-to-last aisle seat—there's a small light over the emergency exit in that area that makes sleeping difficult for me.

"Since food is one of my interests, I'm fussy about airline foods. I'll sometimes take a well-prepared sandwich with me rather than eat the food that's served on certain airlines."

Like most frequent flyers, James Hunt prefers the roominess offered by an aisle seat in first class, but occasionally has to make do with the tourist section. He has learned to make a flight in tourist class as comfortable as possible. "Although you have to take what you can get," he says, "I find that unless the flight is very crowded you can nearly always get an aisle seat with an empty seat between you and the window seat. It's worth asking about, because the reservation agents will normally fill the aisle and window seats first, leaving the middle seats for last. The best possible situation," he continues, "is getting a seat near the back of the plane on a flight that's not crowded. Often, you'll be surrounded by a row of empty seats and you can put up the armrests and spread out. It's better than first class."

If you fly frequently on business, Hunt recommends that you join the clubs offered by the airlines you use most often. "If the plane is sold out in tourist but has seats in first class," he explains, "they'll upgrade the members of the club to first class. That's happened to me a couple of times."

HOTELS

Since the hotel you stay in will be home to you for the duration of your trip, you should choose it carefully. Not all hotels are the same. Some appeal to the business traveler, others to the vacationer, some to status seekers, others people who just want some peace and quiet. Think about your needs before making a reservation. Do you want a hotel that offers secretarial services and an abundance of conference rooms? Or one with cozy rooms and excellent meals? Should it be centrally located, or a bit off the beaten track?

"In any city," says Grunberg, "I like to stay in a hotel that is among the best in town but not the one that's generally regarded as *the* best. I prefer a small hotel, one that feels more like a leisure hotel than a business hotel. I find that more comfortable. In Los Angeles, I stay at L'Hermitage rather than the Bel Air. Before I moved to New York, I stayed in the Regency Hotel or the Westbury Hotel, rather than the Palace or the Plaza, because they're quieter, more understated. In London, I prefer Blake's to the Dorchester or Claridge's. As a general rule, I look for hotels that are not representative of a city's style. I've found that the stylish hotels tend to be too flashy for my taste.

Although Alan Parter looks for the same caliber of hotel as Grunberg, his requirements differ. "I entertain a lot of prospective clients," he says, "and on some trips it's critical that I stay in a flagship hotel. My competition stays in the best places, so I can't be seen in a second- or third-rate hotel.

"The Mandarin in Hong Kong is one of my very favorite hotels. I also like Grosvenor House in London, Il Caviliere in Milan, the Imperial in Tokyo, and the Intercontinental in Frankfurt.

"I need a place that's conveniently located, so that people I'm interested in forming a business relationship with don't have to go out of their way to attend a meeting." Parter's preference for centrally located hotels is also related to the way he likes to spend his leisure time during business trips. "Some people are runners," he says. "I'm a walker. I love to walk for hours in cities, particularly in cities that are new to me. You get a sense of atmosphere, and you get to know the people. One weekend in Hong Kong I found myself, in dress slacks, a white shirt, and a tie, walking down a street and joining in a pickup basketball game. Not only were the other players half my age, they were also half my size. It was one of the best times I've ever had."

RESERVATIONS

When making reservations at any hotel, be as specific as possible. If you're not certain how long your trip will last, book a room for the longest period the trip could possibly take. You'll seldom have any problem with leaving early, but trying to extend a stay at a busy hotel can be impossible.

If you've confirmed a room reservation but arrive to find that there isn't a room for you, stand your ground. Don't create a scene, but make sure the clerk understands that you won't be leaving his desk until you've been accommodated in some fashion. The very least the hotel can do is find you a decent room in a comparable hotel.

For the sake of peace and quiet, request rooms that are away from the elevator banks and avoid those on low floors overlooking traffic-filled streets.

Traveler's Electric Current Adaptors

Don't pay for your stay in advance. If you do, and you're dissatisfied with something, you'll have no leverage when requesting improvements.

163

THE BUSINESSMAN AS TRAVELER

Conducting business in another city, foreign or domestic, is very different from working out of your home office. You're often dealing with people you've never met before, and you need to convey a positive image almost entirely through your appearance and manners.

Clothes are an important part of your image. Experienced business travelers have learned that it's worth paying some attention to the clothes you wear on working trips. "I don't think there's any point in wearing 'controversial' clothing in situations where you don't know people, and don't know how they're going to react," says James Hunt. "In some cities, I won't wear a colored shirt with a white collar. While that's perfectly acceptable business attire in New York, it may not be in the Midwest. And why call attention to something unnecessarily? You can't possibly be criticized for dressing in a subdued fashion."

Leslie Grunberg feels that the business traveler should be appropriately dressed even during the plane trip. "I nearly always dress the same way for travel," he says, "in grey flannel trousers, dress shirt, a blazer, and a tie. I always dress as if I had to go straight to a business meeting from the airport, even if I don't."

"I find conducting business meetings over breakfast in other countries rewarding because they're a uniquely American custom. Your foreign business associates may feel a little uncomfortable at first, but they remember you for them."
—ALAN PARTER

Because Alan Parter travels almost exclusively overseas, he has given particular though to creating a business wardrobe that reflects the image he wants to convey, both personally and as a representative of the United States.

"It may have to do with the fact that I was trained as a lawyer," he says, "but I simply don't feel comfortable in a business environment unless I'm wearing a suit. I'm not comfortable in a sports jacket, even if the people I'm meeting are wearing sports jackets or sweaters. I dress for the standard American style of business, in any country. That's a very deliberate decision, because I feel that look, while conservative, is different enough in many countries to make people remember me.

"I don't want my appearance to be too stern, though, so I've gotten into the habit of wearing colored shirts or 'friendly' ties—bright ties that soften the look of a dark suit and white shirt. I can't tell you how often I have been remembered for wearing colored ties, because most business people don't do that. My practice of wearing bright ties really evolved accidentally. I like colors, and I feel comfortable wearing them. When I realized that the ties had an effect on people, I began making a conscious effort to wear them.

"Ties really are one of the best ways to make a statement. In many countries, it's customary for the host to give the visitor a gift, and one the most popular gifts is the business or locale tie. I must have seven bank ties and ten city or government ties in my collection, and I will bring them along. When I'm in Tokyo, I will wear my City of Tokyo tie. I think that shows planning and concern, and the people I meet there notice and are pleased by it. I will even wear a maple leaf-design tie that I just happened to buy when I go to an office in Toronto.

"My clothes reflect a good blend of formality and comfortable openness, one that makes the people I meet think, 'This guy is here to do business, but he also seems like someone I can talk to.'"

MAKING CONTACT

Once you have your traveling wardrobe in order, you face an even bigger challenge—establishing a rapport with total strangers, a task that's even more difficult in cultures other than your own.

"Different meanings of words can haunt international business relationships," explains Parter, "and the most difficult part is the fact that you may not know when a particular word has been misinterpreted. All too often, people in a meeting will smile knowingly when, in fact, they have no idea what you're saying or, worse, they understand everything but one critical word.

"The problems don't only arise from a language barrier. There's also a usage barrier. Even in England, although we speak the same language, words are sometimes used differently or mean different things in the two countries, and misunderstandings can result from that. At the very least, an Englishman may decide that you're not as bright as he thought you were because by his standards you've used a word incorrectly, although you used it properly by your standards.

"Eventually you learn that you can't let key words and phrases stand alone. You must qualify and explain the words until you're sure your meaning has been clearly understood. The importance of explaining connotations is something I learned only through experience."

In addition to carrying on conversations that are clearly understood by everyone, you have to make sure that your behavior conforms to the standards of the country you're visiting. "I think it's important for any individual who's traveling the world on business to do his homework," Parter says. "You have to try and gain an overview of the place you're going to, both to avoid embarrassing yourself and your host, and to avoid making a major mistake that might kill a deal. I've found that if you make a sincere effort to show your respect, you're likely to be forgiven any small errors you might make. But you have to be flexible. For example, people in some countries like you to ask about their families, people in other countries don't. You have to learn when to recognize the fact that you've made someone uncomfortable with what they consider an inappropriate question, and just move quickly on to another topic.

"The key is really simple etiquette," he says. "That, and being sensitive to other people's feelings. I find that your host doesn't expect you to be just like him, to follow his customs exactly—yet you do want to show your respect for the ways of his country. So you compromise. In an Asian country, for example, I might shake hands with the host when I arrive, but bow, as he does, when I leave. You have to become skillful at sizing up each individual situation, knowing the full range of acceptable behavior, and then choose the behavior that seems most appropriate. Sometimes this means temporarily abandoning American conventions.

"I remember walking down a street in Italy with a man with whom I had just negotiated a deal that was very beneficial to both of us. As we were walking, he took my arm. Intellectually, I knew that it was a completely masculine, comfortable, friendly gesture on his part, but I had an an almost physical reaction to it. I had to consciously restrain myself from pulling away from him, simply because the gesture was so foreign to me. But it was necessary to accept the gesture in the manner it was intended. That doesn't mean that I would take another Italian's arm to show that I was trying to fit into his culture.

"It's important to understand that, in most cases, your host wants to show you the customs of his country. If I'm taken to a restaurant, I don't fight for the check. I think my host very much wants to show me the local wine, the local food, the local chef, and I may offend him by grabbing the check. I simply plan to return the favor if he visits the United States."

Parter had to learn to handle the intricacies of gift giving, a customary part of buiness relationships in many countries, particularly Asia. "It may seem strange to an American businessman, but it's something you have to learn about. Chances are, people you're meeting may present you with a gift, and it's tremendously embarrassing not to have something to give in return," he explains. "Ideally, the gift should reflect both you and the status of the person receiving it. For example, I would not give the same gift to the supervisor of a single department that I would to the chairman of the company. While the gifts would in some way have to do with the United States, both the supervisor and the chairman would be uncomfortable receiving equally prestigious gifts.

"It's not really the cost of the gift that's important," he continues. "It's more its beauty. So I might give the lower-level person a book about the 1980 Winter Olympics held in New York State, and the higher-level person a carving done by a New York artist. Or the lower-level person might receive a paperweight with the governor's signature and the seal of New York, while the higher-level person might receive a piece of Steuben glass made in New York.

"Obviously, these can't be spur-of-the-moment things. You've got to plan carefully before you leave on your trip, and you've got to be prepared to augment the gift you'd planned to give with a dinner or a night at the theater if someone proves particularly helpful and hospitable. Practically speaking, since you have to carry these things around with you until you give them away, you don't want to take anything too heavy or awkwardly shaped. I've received some magnificent art books as gifts and cringed because I knew I had to carry these heavy things around in my suitcase for the rest of the trip."

"I've also learned, over time, to spend an increasing amount of time on creating a social relationship with foreign business contacts," he says. "This is particularly important in Asia, but it also applies in Europe. You have to divorce yourself from the kind of meeting we have in the United States where you say 'Hello, how's your family,' and get right to business without listening to the answer. You may have to force yourself to ask personal questions at first, but the rewards are there. It's enjoyable, and, practically speaking, some Asian and European businessmen simply will not give you all the information you need until they feel comfortable with you personally. They just will not do it. And you can't do your job well until you have all the information."

LUGGAGE

Strength and manageability are the two most important qualities to keep in mind when you're buying luggage. Soft-sided luggage with a shaped inner frame is probably your best choice because it's sturdy, yet lighter than hard-sided luggage. If you're buying a large case, choose one with wheels on the bottom for those times when you can't find a porter. Look for reinforced handles (identifiable by an extra strip of leather around the base of the handle) and a sturdy lock.

If you check your luggage, never put your home address on the bag. The baggage handlers need only your name, destination, and flight number. They're not interested in anything else—but a passing burglar might be. Attach your business card to the inside of the bag. If the bag goes astray, the airline will identify it from that.

HOW TO PACK

Whether you're packing a compact carry-on bag or full-sized suitcase, the rules remain basically the same. You want to make your clothing conform to the shape of your luggage with as few folds as possible, because folds can result in wrinkles.

To fold clothes carefully for packing, you'll need a few sheets of nonacid tissue paper. If you use it to line trouser, vest, jacket, sweater, and shirt folds, you'll minimize unwanted creases and wrinkles. Using tissue for packing is not time-consuming. There are two types of tissue available, acid and nonacid. The nonacid is the best choice because it's the sturdiest, purest white, and the more practical of the two. (You can find it at most dime stores and notions shops. It's inexpensive.)

Another way to fight wrinkles is to cover individual garments, after they've been folded, with light plastic dry-cleaner bags.

Frank Hurd, one of London's leading caterers, served for several years as butler to a British ambassador. He once worked as a footman at St. Michael's Mount, a fabled island castle off England's Cornish coast. "One of the first things I was taught by the butler in residence, Stanley Ager, was how to fold and pack clothes so that they would be crease-free, regardless of how long they stayed packed. Mr. Ager claimed that he folded his serving clothes and laid them in a trunk in 1939 when entered military service. When he returned some six years later at the end of World War II, he opened the trunk, gave his morning coat a single shake, slipped into it and moments later oversaw the family dinner without a wrinkle. The key to proper folding and packing is to preserve the natural folds of the arms, the waist line, and the seams."

"When I travel, I leave my shirts and suits in the plastic wraps and pouches that they are in when they come back from the cleaners. It cushions them with air and they don't crush as badly."
—FRANK GIAMBRONE,
Senior executive vice president, sales,
Jacqueline Cochran, Inc.

HOW FRANK HURD FOLDS A SUIT

Begin by laying the suit flat on a bed or table.

*To fold a jacket for a large grip
or standard suitcase:*

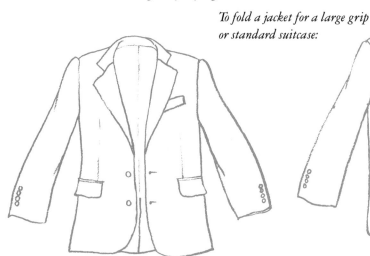

1. Lay the unbuttoned jacket face up, with its collar flat and its shoulders squared.

2. Pull the buttonholes of the jacket over the buttons, overlapping them by five or six inches. The side seams should lie smoothly in a straight line.

3. Fold one sleeve across the lapel, bringing its hem to the opposite shoulder. The jacket should still lie flat, not pull up at the armhole.

4. Fold the other sleeve across the first, bringing its hem to the opposite shoulder. Make sure the jacket is still lying flat.

5. Fold the jacket in half by bringing its bottom up to the shoulder. Gently arrange the outer edged of the jacket so they cover the sleeves.

To fold a jacket for a small grip:

This technique preserves the jacket's natural waistline and seam folds while making as slim a package as possible.

1. Empty out the pockets. Lay the jacket flat, lining-side down. Turn the collar up so it lies flat. (It's reinforced, so it won't crease.)

2. Fold up both sleeves at the elbow so the tip of the cuffs reach the outside edge of the shoulders.

3. Turn back the sides of the jacket to the center back seam, which should just be visible between them.

4. Fold the jacket along the center back seam, bringing the lapels together. The jacket is now long and thin, and there is a natural fold under each armhole.

5. Fold up at the waist. To make it fit your grip, tuck in any extra material from the coattails between the folds of the jacket.

To fold a vest:

1. Unbutton the vest and lay it flat, right side up.

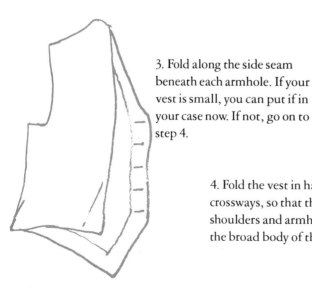

2. Fold it along the back seam from top to bottom to preserve the natural fold under each armhole. The two lower points will overlap.

3. Fold along the side seam beneath each armhole. If your vest is small, you can put if in your case now. If not, go on to step 4.

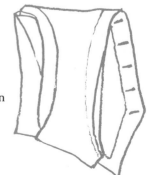

4. Fold the vest in half crossways, so that the shoulders and armholes lie on the broad body of the vest.

To fold a shirt:

If you're packing a clean shirt just back from the laundry, it's already perfectly folded. If the shirt has been washed and pressed at home, you can fold it as well as the professionals do by following the steps below.

1. Fasten the middle button and lay the shirt face down on a table or bed.

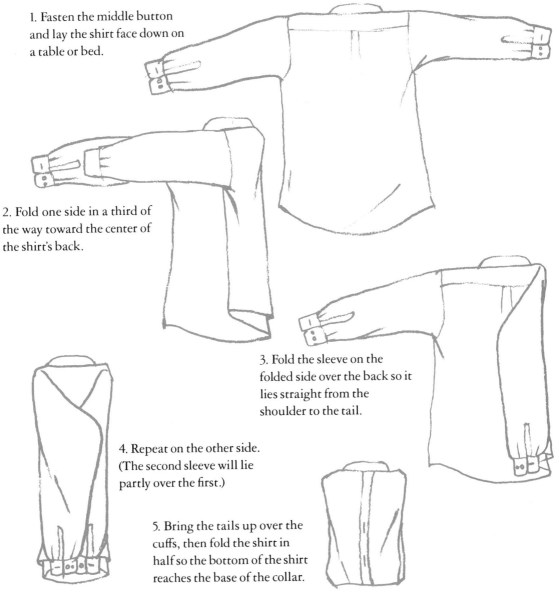

2. Fold one side in a third of the way toward the center of the shirt's back.

3. Fold the sleeve on the folded side over the back so it lies straight from the shoulder to the tail.

4. Repeat on the other side. (The second sleeve will lie partly over the first.)

5. Bring the tails up over the cuffs, then fold the shirt in half so the bottom of the shirt reaches the base of the collar.

To fold trousers:

1. Trousers should be folded at the base of the seat when you take them off the hanger, so you need only lay them flat, empty the pockets, and fold the linings away from the creases to preserve them.

2. If you're wide through the waist, fold the back of the waistband down and toward the front at an angle, as illustrated.

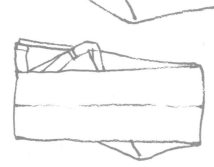

3. Fold the bottom of the trousers up to meet the waistband.

To fold jeans:

You can treat jeans exactly as you would a pair of dress trousers. But because they're so sturdy, you can save space by aligning the legs and rolling them from the waist all the way down to the cuffs. (This method is especially handy for small carry-on bags, or for filling gaps in a larger suitcase.)

To fold a sweater:

It's perfectly all right to fold a sweater exactly as you would a shirt, but if you're trying to conserve space the method given below results in a smaller package.

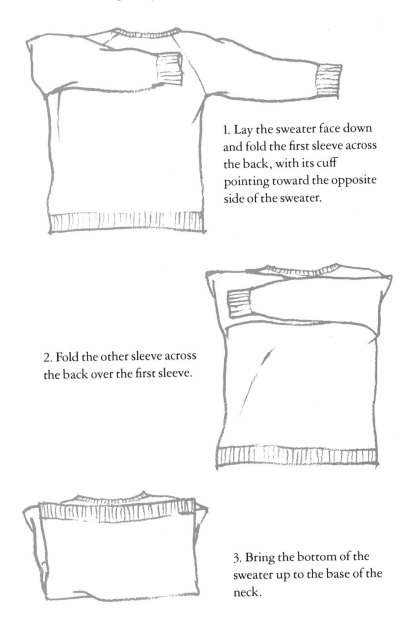

1. Lay the sweater face down and fold the first sleeve across the back, with its cuff pointing toward the opposite side of the sweater.

2. Fold the other sleeve across the back over the first sleeve.

3. Bring the bottom of the sweater up to the base of the neck.

To fold two ties together:

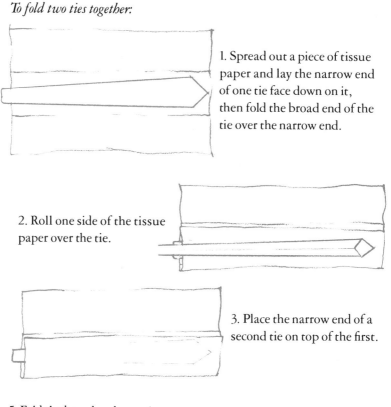

1. Spread out a piece of tissue paper and lay the narrow end of one tie face down on it, then fold the broad end of the tie over the narrow end.

2. Roll one side of the tissue paper over the tie.

3. Place the narrow end of a second tie on top of the first.

5. Fold the broad end over the narrow end and roll the other side of the tissue paper over the second tie.

When the garments are folded, use them to create flat, fairly tightly packed layers of clothing, one on top of the other, until the case is filled. (If there is a lot of empty space in the case, the folded items will shift about and wrinkle, so make sure to fill gaps with underwear and socks.)

PACKING A GARMENT BAG

Make sure you leave some room between the clothes in the bag or they're sure to crush. The flimsy sides of the bag offer little protection.

Suits: Hang trousers, vest and jacket together on one hanger (vest over trousers, jacket over vest). Center the trousers on the hanger with the waistband hanging nearly a foot below the bar. Bring the buttonholes on both the vest and the jacket about a third of the way across the button sides to make them fit in the bag without folding or creases.

Trousers and Jeans: You can hang two pairs of trousers on one hanger by arranging them so the waistbands hang on opposite sides of the hanger.

Shirts, Sweaters, and Ties: You can fold these as you would for any other bag and place them in the side pockets of the garment bag.

Shaving Kit: The bag offers little protection from rough handling, so the best place for this (or any other potentially breakable items) is in the corner of the bag near the handle.

CARRY YOUR COAT

If you're bringing a coat with you, a trench coat is a better choice than a bulky top coat. Worn over a sweater, a trench coat will provide protection in even the coldest climates, and it will recover nicely from the rough handling it may have to endure on the airplane. "I always fold my trench coat and put it on the overhead rack," frequent business traveler Carlton Thompson says. "I would never use the closet on the plane, because the airlines are still using these little sawed-off children's sized hangers that don't extend to the edge of the shoulders. At the end of the flight you've got two big ridges in your coat. I wouldn't put a coat on a tiny hanger at home, so I'm not going to do it on the plane."

TRAVELER'S CHECKLIST

- Save time by using carry-on luggage whenever possible.

- Plan your flight carefully, making sure to specify the smoking or nonsmoking section, as well as an aisle or window seat. Confirm your seat reservation two days before departure.

- Telephone the airport before leaving your home or office to make sure that your flight is on schedule.

- Leave yourself plenty of time to get to the airport, to minimize stress and the possibility of being bumped from your flight.

- Pack clothing to minimize creases and conserve space.

- Choose a hotel that offers the facilities you'll need during your stay.

- Make sure you have all your paperwork—passport, visa, medical prescriptions—in order before you leave.

- Carry traveler's checks instead of cash, a two-way dictionary, a map, and a pocket calculator.

- When conducting business in a foreign city, learn and respect the customs of your hosts.

THE
ENTERTAINER

Entertaining may very well have begun at that first garden get-together: "Have an apple?" Admittedly, the guest list was short and the party didn't end as well as it might have (all that lightning and thunder and loud voices and then having to locate a different garden for the next get-together) but it was a start. We've come a long way since then. Today, it's much easier to ensure that the experience will have a happy ending and leave a pleasant emotional aftertaste.

Successful hosting springs largely from attitude. A thoughtful host knows the event is an opportunity to show his respect for his guests, and that the best way to do that is by paying attention to details. Whether it's a small dinner at home for good friends or a restaurant sortie with business associates, the responsibilities of the host are the same. In short, you become the "cruise director" and it's up to you to see that the occasion is relaxed and easy and pleasantly memorable for all. This is where an eye for detail becomes so important—the success of any gathering is in direct relation to the amount of planning and necessary staging that goes into it. This allows you to free yourself and your guests from distraction for a few hours and get on with the pleasures of being together.

THE HOST AT A RESTAURANT

If you'd like to entertain your friends or business associates with a minimum of fuss, a good restaurant can solve all your problems. But few men know how to get the most out of a restaurant.

"I think the biggest mistake you can make when you go into a restaurant is to try and order people around, to demand certain things, in order to show how much you know about wines and food," says Phil Scotty, owner of Manhattan's Century Café and Café Lui. "If you're knowledgeable, terrific. That just means you can make good choices. Every once in a while, you run into the guy who sends back three bottles of wine. He's trying to impress somebody, but nobody's impressed. Smart people use restaurants as an extension of their home or office. They come in and make it their own. It doesn't matter if it's the first time you've been in a restaurant or the tenth—use it. It's a place to sit down and have dinner. It's a place to meet a friend for some casual conversation. It's a place to do business. It's a place to make social contact. It's an extension of your world. Don't make it something outside of that. Don't make it a test. It's not a test. I think most people believe that they have to act in an acceptable manner, that there's an unwritten restaurant bible that says you have to be cool when you walk into a restaurant. You have to be yourself. If people pretended that a table in a restaurant was the coffee table in their living room, they would enjoy themselves more. It's only a restaurant, it's not the World Series."

"When you're looking for a good restaurant, word-of-mouth and reviews by food critics are both informative, but you shouldn't let yourself be discouraged from visiting a place you've always wanted to try. Firsthand experience is the best."
—VINCENT SARDI, *restaurateur*

First and foremost, remember that you're not simply buying your friends a meal. You're trying to give them a pleasant evening out, so you need to pay attention to more than food. You want to take them to a place that has a congenial atmosphere and efficient, attractive service. If you have a favorite restaurant that fits that description, fine. If you don't have a specific place in mind, however, ask a knowledgeable friend for recommendations. Get the names of a few places and visit them yourself well in advance of the event to sample their ambience and service. Choose a restaurant that complements the mood of your party, whether it be a raucous country-and-western bar or an elegant French café.

"From my observation," says writer and food critic Jay Jacobs, "most people are uncomfortable walking into any restaurant. And that's not as it should be. You're paying good money for an evening's entertainment, and going to a restaurant shouldn't make you any more uncomfortable than going to a theater or a concert."

You'll reduce that level of discomfort if you take the time to get to know—and be known by—restaurants.

"When a popular restaurant doesn't know you," says food and restaurant writer Mimi Sheraton, "it's best to call well in advance to get a reservation for the time you want. You're most likely to get the time you want on the least busy night, so plan your first few visits for Tuesdays, Wednesdays, or Thursdays. Some very in restaurants may be adamant about not giving you any time between six and nine, because they prefer to save the more popular dinner hours for regular customers. You can try saying 'that's unreasonable for our plans, when is the first date we can come at 7:30?' If they say 'never,' I just wouldn't bother with them anymore.

"It's almost impossible to buy a table from the maître d' with a $10 bill. An honorable owner will fire a maître d' for selling tables."
—SHELLY FIREMAN, *restaurateur*

"You can sometimes avoid those problems by frequenting the restaurant at lunch," she continues. "It's usually possible to get reservations for the times you want at lunch, and the staff will get to know you then, making it easier to get dinner reservations. That's really not entirely snobbery—people just can't help being a little warmer and friendlier to people they know. They should, of course, be nice to everyone."

When you call for evening reservations, ask who you're speaking to. It helps, if you're speaking to a principle of the restaurant, to say something that may make a difference to them. You can say that you've always heard about the place, that you're bringing a friend for a special occasion, and you're really looking forward to it. Things like that sometimes register with the more decent people. Once you're there, you may find that you don't like the table they've given you because it's near the kitchen or bathroom door. You can ask to have it changed, but if the restaurant is busy you might be stuck with it. You can leave, or you can stay there and make a point of telling the maître d' on the way out, "we had a wonderful time and we'd love to come back, but how can we avoid getting that table again?" If the restaurant really did please you and you want to go back, that's the time to slip the maître d' money to make sure he remembers you. Chances are, your table will be better next time.

Jay Jacobs advocates a slightly more agressive approach. "I think that one thing that any diner can do, if he's offered a really poor table somewhere off in left field, is march over and take a look at the reservation log to see where his name appears in the sequence. If it's down there early enough, he's got every right to demand a better table."

Dressing to conform to restaurant standards is a simple courtesy that can make your meal more pleasant. "When you go to any restaurant," says Mimi Sheraton, "I believe you should be conservatively dressed by their standards. I don't believe that you should act any differently from the way you normally do, but there's no point in 'testing' a restaurant by walking in without a tie, or shoes, or whatever. When you phone for a reservation, ask if they have a dress code. If they do, abide by it. If you don't want to abide by it, don't go. A restaurant owner is entitled to make his own rules, as long as they're the same for everyone."

Jay Jacobs believes a good restaurant depends on more than the quality of the food. "A diner has every right to be greeted cordially and seated decently if he's made a reservation far enough in advance —I don't think he should be shunted off to the worst table in the house simply because he happens to be an unknown newcomer. I think he can expect courteous, prompt service without too much conversational intrusion from the waiters. Good food in pleasant surroundings is essential. I think what matters to me more than anything is what I can only call the totality of the experience. I want to go to a restaurant and have a good time, a festive evening. I find myself disliking a number of restaurants where the atmosphere is too solemn. All the emphasis is placed on the quality of the food, in some cases the esoteric nature of the food, and an evening out becomes something like a high requiem mass. I want to laugh a little."

A little research is in order before you visit any restaurant for the first time. You'll be more comfortable in a new restaurant if you can learn a little bit about the restaurant in advance, or about the kinds of dishes they specialize in. You'll feel less pressure when you're reading the menu, especially if the captain is standing there, and he's busy, he's trying to rush you, and you're trying to decipher the French menu.

"I think it's ridiculous for a restaurant in the United States to have a menu written only in French," notes Mimi Sheraton. "Too often, the captain will mention one or two daily specials, and the shy diner will take one of those or ask for a steak rather than say 'what's this dish, and what is this dish, and what is this dish,' until he understands the whole menu and can choose what he'd really like. But you're not going to get your money's worth if you let yourself be hustled into the first thing that you can remember. I think that the diner should say to the captain, 'I'm sorry to have to ask you to do this, but we've never been here before, and I'd like to know what all these dishes are. Could you explain?' Since the menu is all in French, it's really the restaurant's fault that the captain has to spend his time that way."

"When I'm looking for a good restaurant in a strange town, I'll go outside and watch people just walking along. When I see someone who looks like I would like him if I knew him, I'll ask him to recommend a place."
—PHIL SCOTTY, *restaurateur*

Jacobs suggests that diners acquaint themselves with the foreign terminology most often found on menus in order to reduce menu anxiety. "I think that three out of any five people in any restaurant don't know what they've got in their hands when they look at a menu. If the menu is in a foreign language, they're at a terrific disadvantage. But they don't have to be—this ignorance isn't something that takes years to overcome. You can familiarize yourself with the classics in three or four languages in pretty short order."

Jacobs' book *Winning The Restaurant Game* offers a comprehensive list of menu terminology, definitions, and pronounciation; what follows is a sampling of the most often used terms.

FRENCH

AGNEAU: *lamb*
AIL: *garlic*
AÏOLI: *garlic mayonnaise*
A LA CARTE: *each item is billed separately*
AUX AMANDES/ AMANDINE: *with almonds*
BALLOTINE: *boneless meat or fish poached in its skin*
BÉARNAISE: *a sauce of butter, egg yolks, herbs, vinegar, and wine*
BISQUE: *puréed soup*
BOEUF: *beef*
BOUDIN: *blood sausage*
BOUILLABAISSE: *fish stew*
BRAISÉ: *braised*
BRIOCHE: *a soft roll or bun, sometimes filled with meat*
CAFÉ: *coffee*
CANARD: *duck*
CARRÉ: *rib roast*
CASSOULET: *casserole, usually containing white beans and meat*

CERVELLES: *brains*
CHAMPIGNONS: *mushrooms*
CHARCUTERIE: *assorted cooked meat*
CHATEAUBRIAND: *a thick slice of beef filet, often served with béarnaise sauce*
CONSOMMÉ: *clarified soup*
COQ: *chicken*
COQ AU VIN: *chicken in red wine*
COQUILLE: *shell*
COQUILLES ST.-JACQUES: *scallops in sauce, served in a scallop shell*
CORDON BLEU: *refers to the practice of stuffing veal or chicken with ham and cheese, then breading and sautéing*
CÔTE: *chop*
CRÈME: *cream*
CRÊPE: *a thin pancake, often folded over a filling*

CROÛTE, en: *wrapped in pastry*
CRUDITÉs: *raw vegetables, often served with sauces and dips as an hors d'oeuvre*
DAUBE: *a stew that usually contains beef and red wine*
DEMI: *half*
DÉSOSSÉ: *boneless*
DIJONNAISE: *with mustard sauce*
DINDE: *turkey*
DODINE: *breast of fowl*
DUCHESSE, À LA: *with browned mashed potatoes*
DUXELLES: *chopped mushrooms sautéed with onions*
ENTRECÔTE: *"between the ribs," a sirloin steak*
ENTREMETS: *desserts*
ESCARGOTS: *snails*
FAISAN: *pheasant*
FARCI: *stuffed*
FLAMBÉ: *flamed*
FLAN: *fruit tart*
FOIE: *liver*
FOIE GRAS: *liver of goose or duck*
FOUR, AU: *oven baked*
FRAÎCHE/FRAIS: *fresh*
FRAISES: *strawberries*
FRAMBOISES: *raspberries*
FRICASSÉE: *stewed poultry in white sauce*
FRIT/FRITE: *fried*
FROID: *cold*
FROMAGE: *cheese*
FUMÉ: *smoked*
GARNI: *garnished*
GÂTEAU: *cake*
GENOISE: *sponge cake*

GIBIER: *game*
GIGOT: *leg of lamb*
GLACE: *ice cream*
GRATIN: *topped with grated, browned cheese*
GRENOUILLES: *frogs' legs*
GRILLADES: *grilled meats*
HACHÉ: *chopped*
HOLLANDAISE: *a sauce of butter, egg yolks, and lemon juice*
HOMARD: *lobster*
HUITRES: *oysters*
INDIENNE, À L': *curried or highly spiced*
JAMBON: *ham*
JARDINIÈRE: *garnished with vegetables*
JUS: *juice*
LAIT: *milk*
LAITUE: *lettuce*
LANGOUSTE: *spiny lobster*
LANGOUSTINES: *crawfish*
LARD: *bacon*
LENTILLES: *lentils*
LYONNAISE: *with onions*
MÂCONNAISE, À LA: *prepared with red wine*
MAINTENON: *a sauce of cream and egg yolks*
MAISON/À LA MAISON: *in the style of the house*
MARINÈRE: *marinated*
MÉDAILLON: *a thick round slice of beef or veal*
MEUNIÈRE: *dredged in flour, sautéed, with lemon butter and parsley*
MOELLE: *marrow*
MORILLE: *morel, a wild mushroom*

MOULES: *mussels*
MOUTARDE: *mustard*
MOUTON: *mutton*
NATUR/NATUREL, AU: *plain, no garnishes*
NIÇOISE: *as in Nice, usually contains black olives, anchovies, and garlic*
NOUILLES: *Noodles*
OEUF: *egg*
OIGNON: *onion*
PAIN: *bread*
PALOURDES: *clams*
PAPILLOTE, EN: *baked in paper*
PATISSERIES: *pastries*
PÊCHE: *peach*
PIEDS DE PORC: *pig's feet*
POCHÉ: *poached*
POIRE: *pear*
POISSON: *fish*
POIVRE: *pepper*
POMME: *apple*
POMMES DE TERRE: *potatoes*
PORC: *pork*
POTAGE: *soup*
POULARDE: *roasting chicken*
POULET: *broiling chicken*
PRIX FIXE: *one price for the complete meal*
PROVENÇALE, À LA: *made with olive oil, garlic, or tomatoes (or all three)*
QUENELLES: *poached dumplings of meat, fowl, or fish*
RATATOUILLE: *a vergetable stew*
RIZ: *rice*
ROGNONS: *kidneys*
ROSBIF: *roast beef*

RÔTI: *roasted*
SAIGNANT: *rare, bloody*
SAUMON: *salmon*
SERVICE COMPRIS: *a service charge is included in the bill, so no tipping is required.*
SORBET: *sherbet*
TARTARE: *served raw*
THÉ: *tea*
THON: *tuna*
TOMATE: *tomato*
TRUITE: *trout*
VAPEUR, À LA: *steamed*
VEAU: *veal*
VIANDES: *meats*
VICHYSSOISE: *a soup of potato, leek, and cream or milk. Often served cold*
VIN: *wine*

ITALIAN

A/AI/ALLA/ALL': *in the style of*
AL: *with*
AFFOGATO: *steamed*
AFFUMATO: *smoked*
AGLIO: *garlic*
AGNELLO: *lamb*
ALFREDO, FETTUCINE: *egg noodles in butter and cheese sauce*
ANITRA: *duck*
ANTIPASTO/ANTIPASTI: *appetizers*
ARAGOSTA: *lobster*
ARROSTO: *roasted*
BASILICO: *basil*
BIANCO: *white*
BISTECCA: *Beefsteak*
BOLLITO: *boiled*
BRASATO: *braised*
BRODETTO: *broth*
BRODO: *broth*
BURRO: *butter*
CAFFÉ: *coffee*
CALAMARI: *squid*
CANNELLONI: *pasta tubes filled with meat or cheese*
CANNOLI: *a sweet pastry*
CAPONATA: *vegetable stew*
CAPELLE DE FUNGHI: *mushroom caps*
CAPPUCCINO: *strong coffee with steamed milk added*
CARBONARA: *a sauce of bacon, cheese, and egg yolks*
CARNE: *meat*
CASSOLA, IN: *cooked and served in a casserole*

CAVIALE: *caviar*
CERVELLE: *brains*
CIPOLLE: *onions*
CONIGLIO: *rabbit*
COPERTO: *cover charge*
COZZE: *mussels*
CREMA: *custard*
CROSTATA: *tart*
CRUDO: *raw*
DENTE, AL: *firm to the bite, i.e. pasta*
DOLCE: *sweets, dessert*
FAGIOLI: *beans*
FEGATINI: *chicken livers*
FEGATO: *liver*
FERRI, AL: *grilled*
FILETTO: *fillet*
FONDUTA: *cheese fondue*
FORMAGGIO: *cheese*
FRA DIAVOLO: *crusteaceans, usually lobster, sautéed and served in a sauce of tomatoes, garlic oil, wine, onion, and hot pepper*
FRAGOLE: *strawberries*
FREDDO: *cold*
FRESCA: *fresh, raw*
FRITTATA: *omelet*
FRITTO: *fried*
FRUTTA: *fruit*
FRUTTI DE MARE: *seafood*
FUNGHI: *mushrooms*
GAMBE DE RANE: *frogs' legs*
GAMBERI: *shrimp*
GAMBERO: *crawfish*
GELATI: *ice cream*
GNOCCHI: *small dumplings, usually containing potatoes*
GRANCHIO: *crab*
GRANITE: *ices*

GRATINATE: *topped with grated, browned cheese*
GRIGLIA: *grilled*
GRISSINI: *breadsticks*
IMBOTTITO: *stuffed*
INSALATA: *salad*
LATTE: *milk*
LATTUGA: *lettuce*
LENTICCHIE: *lentils*
LIMONE: *lemon*
LOMBATINA: *filet steak*
LUCIANA, SALSA: *a sauce of garlic, tomatoes, olive oil, and white wine*
LUGÁNA: *a spicy pork sausage*
LUMACHE: *snails*
MAIALE: *pork*
MANZO: *beef*
MARINARA: *a sauce of tomatoes, oil, garlic, and parsley*
MEDAGLIONE: *a small round slice of meat*
MINESTRE: *soups*
MINESTRONE: *a thick vegetable soup*
MOLECHE: *softshell crabs*
OLIO: *oil, usually olive*
OREGANATE: *seasoned with oregano*
OSSOBUCO: *braised veal shank*
OSTRICHE: *oysters*
PANE: *bread*
PANNA: *cream*
PASTICCERIA: *pastry*
PATATA: *potato*
PEPE: *pepper*
PEPERONCINI: *chili peppers*
PESCE: *fish*
PESTO: *sauce of basil, olive oil, and garlic*

PICCANTE: *spicy*
PIGNOLI: *pine nuts*
POLLO: *chicken*
POLPO: *octopus*
POMODORO: *tomato*
PRIMAVERA: *containing fresh vegetables*
PROSCUITTO: *cured ham*
RIPIENE: *stuffed*
RISO: *rice*
ROGNONI: *kidneys*
ROSMARINO: *rosemary*
ROSSO: *red*
SALAME: *salami*
SALSA: *sauce*
SALTATO: *sautéed*
SARDE: *sardines*
SCALOPPINE: *slices of veal, pounded thin*
SCAMPI: *shrimp sautéed in butter and garlic*
SCRIPPELLE: *crêpes*
SCUNGILLI: *conch*
SELVAGGINA: *game*
SOGLIO: *sole*
STRACOTTO: *pot roast*
STUFATO: *stew*
SUCCO: *juice*
SUGO, AL: *with meat gravy or sauce*
SUPREMA: *breast of fowl*
TÉ: *tea*
TORTA: *tart*
TROTA: *trout*
UOVA: *eggs*
VERDE: *green*
VINO: *wine*
VONGOLE: *clams*
ZABAGLIONE: *a dessert custard*
ZUPPA: *soup*

SPANISH/MEXICAN

ABONDIGAS DE CARNE: *meatballs*
ABONDIGON: *meatloaf*
ALMEJAS: *clams*
ALUBIAS: *beans*
ANGULAS: *eels*
ARROZ: *rice*
ASADO: *roasted*
ATUN: *tuna*
BIZCOCHO: *sponge cake*
BLANCO: *white*
CALAMARES: *squid*
CALDO: *broth*
CALLOS: *tripe*
CAMARONES/GAMBAS: *shrimp*
CARACOLES: *snails*
CAZUELA, EN: *in a casserole*
CERDO: *pork*
CHILES RELLENOS: *stuffed peppers*
CHORIZO: *pork sausage*
CHULETA: *chop*
COCHINILLO: *suckling pig*
CORDERO: *lamb*
CREMA: *cream custard or pastry filling*
EMPANADA: *meat or vegetables fried in pastry*
ENSALADA: *salad*

ESCABECHE: *marinated*
ESTOFADO: *stew*
FILETE: *fillet*

FLAN: *caramel custard dessert*
FORNO, AL: *oven roasted*
FRIJOLES: *beans*
FRITO: *fried*
GALLINA: *stewing chicken*
GARBANZOS: *chickpeas*
HIGADILLOS DE POLLO: *chicken livers*
HUEVOS: *eggs*
JAMÓN: *ham*
JEREZ: *sherry*
JUGO: *juice*
LANGOSTA: *lobster*
LECHE: *milk*
LENGUADO: *sole*
MAHONESA: *mayonnaise*
MARISCOS: *seafood*
MEJILLONES: *mussels*
NARANJA: *orange*
OSTRAS: *oysters*
PAN: *bread*
PARRILLA, A LA: *grilled*
PATATAS: *potatoes*
PATO: *duck*
PESCADOS: *fish*
PUERCO: *pork*
RELLENO: *stuffed*
SALSA: *sauce*
SALTEADA: *sautéed*
SOLOMILLO: *sirloin*
SOPA: *soup*
TAPAS: *appetizers*
TERNERA: *veal*
TRUCHA: *trout*
VIEIRAS: *sea scallops*

AT EASE IN A RESTAURANT

There's a great deal of unfamiliarity on the part of restaurantgoers with the dining-room hierarchy. They often don't know who they're dealing with, whether it's the maître d', the owner, the captain, the waiter, or the busboy. Because of this, they tend to be much more intimidated by the staff than they should be.

The maître d' is there to welcome and seat you. He can usually be recognized by his formal attire. He's often mistaken for the owner, a foolish error since the owner will usually wear an ordinary business suit. The captain is the head of the service team responsible for your table and the amenities and comforts thereof. He will announce the day's specials and present the wine list (unless there is a sommelier, or wine steward). The waiter will take your order and bring your food. The busboys will clear dishes and replace ashtrays.

To get a good idea of a restaurant's capabilities, Jay Jacobs says he will often order a simple consommé. "I don't think you can get an accurate idea of what the kitchen can do by ordering the costly delicacies like caviar or smoked salmon or foie gras in most cases," he says. "Chances are, some guy in the back opens a package and serves it. You can do that just as well as he can at home. But a consommé, if done properly, can be one of the most satisfying things in the world, and it gives you a good idea of what the kitchen crew can do."

"I don't care whether I get one of the so-called best tables in the house. I don't care where they put me as long as I'm not being treated to a show of contempt."
—JAY JACOBS, *food writer*

Mimi Sheraton agrees that the simple foods are often the best test. "Roast chicken is a good choice," she says. "It's simple, but so few restaurants do it well." She adds that the chefs she knows favor simple foods such as chicken, fish, and eggs when they cook for themselves.

When you're choosing a restaurant for a specific occasion, a few general criteria apply:

1. Look for a fairly extensive menu to ensure that all of your guests will find something they like.

2. Choose a convenient location. Don't force all of your guests to travel miles from home.

3. Make sure that the seating, lighting, rest room locations, and other amenities will be suitable for all your guests—older people probably won't be comfortable sitting on the floor of a Japanese restaurant, and handicapped or injured people may require a restaurant that's easily accessible by wheelchair.

4. Check the glassware and cutlery. There's no excuse for spotted tableware. Ask the waiter to replace it immediately. If he doesn't, or argues, cross that restaurant off your list.

5. Make sure that your meal is prepared to your specifications. If you order a medium-rare steak and it arrives charred, send it back. If the waiter doesn't remove it promptly and courteously, remove that restaurant from your list.

Once you've chosen a restaurant you're sure your guests will enjoy, make sure you let the restaurant know that you're planning a party there. Don't just appear with eight guests and expect everything to go smoothly. Instead, make reservations as far in advance as possible. Give the maître d' the exact time and number of guests, and let him know if you'd prefer a particular location, such as a table by the window. Tell him if you want special arrangements for music or flowers. Make sure you put the reservation in your own name so your guests will know whose table to ask for.

"When I have a business lunch out of town, if it's at my invitation, I want to be the one to choose the restaurant and make the arrangements. And I usually do this well in advance."
—FRANK GIAMBRONE,
Senior executive vice president, sales, Jacqueline Cochran, Inc.

When the party is under way, conduct yourself very much the way you would in your own home. Be polite to restaurant staff—you can't expect them to be courteous if you're rude—but don't be intimidated. If menus are presented before you're ready to order, ask that they be taken away. When you are ready to order, it's the host's responsibility to ask about house specials that may not appear on the menu, and to ask each of his guests what they want and order for them.

If wine is called for, it's your responsibiility as the host to order it, either from the waiter or, if a wine steward is present, directly from him. If the food order is mixed—fish, fowl, veal, and beef—you may want to involve the wine steward in the discussion. Unless money is no object, ask for suggestions concerning types of wines, not specific bottles. If you're not clear about what you're looking for, the steward will probably take you to the top of the line and you'll find yourself stuck with a costlier wine than the meal requires.

Wine expert Lucio Sorre, the chief wine taster of Villa Banfi, USA, the nation's largest wine importer, has his own system for cross-ordering. "If someone at a table of four orders poached trout, someone orders a bland chicken dish, someone orders a grilled veal chop, and someone orders steak au poivre," Sorre says, "the best thing to do is split the order. White wine can complement the chicken and the trout, so those two people can share a bottle of white wine that's not bone dry. They might try a chenin blanc, fumé blanc, sauvignon blanc, soave, dry vouvray, muscadet, or maçon blanc.

"Wine is meant to be enjoyed with food. You cannot possibly drink wine all night without food. In recent years, some California winemakers have specialized in making overly poweful and intense 'monolith' wines—they're like the huge stone figures on Easter Island. They are awesome and impressive, but hardly vivacious or convivial dining companions."
—LUCIO SORRE, *Villa Banfi*

"The steak au poivre calls for a massive red wine, but it shouldn't be ordered because it would annihilate the veal dish. You can compromise with a pinot noir or cabernet sauvignon from from California, or a chianti clasico riserva from Italy, or a Côtes du Beaune from France.

"If you are going to order only one wine, then you have to choose one that does not quite disappear with the most intense dish and does not quite annihilate the least flavorful dish. The catch-all wine would be a light red. Light red has more complexity and, even though it will not sit well with the poached trout, it will not really erase it. You could try a valpolicella from Italy, or a young California red. In this situation, perhaps the best solution is for the person having the blandest dish to get one or two glasses of wine from the bar, and let the others share a bottle.

"Years ago, when people were faced with this decision, they were intimidated and would say 'give us a beer,' or 'give us another drink.' A distillate will never do justice to any food, and beer will do justice only to certain foods that are, let's say, picnic foods. But elaborate foods are not enhanced by drinking beer."

When it's time to pay, either accompany the waiter to the desk or pay with a credit card. Your guests shouldn't be made to feel guilty over how much you've spent.

TIPPING

Tipping is something of a moral obligation. When you walk into any restaurant, unless there is a set service charge, you know there's a mutual understanding that tipping is part of staff subsidization. If you patronize a given restaurant fairly regularly, keep your tipping policy consistent. Don't get wildly overgenerous one night just because you happen to be in a good mood, because that generosity is going to be expected every time thereafter.

Keep tips to a minimum if service is really poor, and let your conscience be your guide if it's really good. Tip a little more generously if some special pains have been taken—if a bottle of wine has been knocked over and the cleanup is gracefully handled, that merits a generous tip. If a member of your party is making a general nuisance of himself and it's taken in good grace by the waiter or the captain, you should be inclined to get a little more generous but not so far out of a given boundary that excessive generosity is going to be expected every time you come in from then on.

Those general boundaries would be 15 to 20 percent of the total bill for the waiter, 5 percent for the captain, and anywhere from two to five dollars for the maître d', but only if he's gone out of his way to be helpful. You needn't tip him if he only checks your reservation and shows you your table. Never try to bribe your way to a good table. In some places that won't be tolerated—the maître d' simply won't accept your money. And even if he does, chances are

"When you ask a waiter, 'what do you recommend?' and his answer is 'everything is good,' you might as well leave."
—VINCENT SARDI, *restaurateur*

193

he'll feel a certain contempt for you—trying to buy a table betrays a lack of savoir-faire.

A wine steward should be given between 10 and 12 percent of the wine bill. It's his responsibility to be available to receive his tip when you're ready to leave. The bartender should receive 15 percent of the bar bill.

THE HOST AT HOME

When you're hosting a party, remember to tailor it to suit the number of guests you plan to invite, the size of your home, the state of your tableware, your skill in the kitchen, and your budget. There's a style of party to suit every occasion.

"When you're entertaining at home," says Mimi Sheraton, "You should do things that really express you, things that you know you can do well. Too often, people feel they have to do what I call 'restaurant dishes' when company is coming. It' very difficult to duplicate restaurant dishes at home, because restaurants have many people at different stations to do each task. One makes the sauce, one cooks the vegetables—there are about six people getting all the food on the plate at the right time. It's simply not practical for the average host to assume that he can do that all alone or with one other person in the kitchen."

"I prefer to give small parties. Then I can choose the right chemistries between people and invite friends who will enjoy and appreciate one another's conversation. And, selfishly, a small gathering means that I can join in on the interesting conversations. In a very large group, you sort of lose control."
—GEOFFREY BEENE

When you're planning any kind of party, make choices that you feel comfortable with. *Don't* try to duplicate what you may have seen pictured in books or magazines, unless it's something you honestly think you can do well, with a minimum of anxiety.

Mimi Sheraton offers an excellent example of translating personal style to entertaining: "I remember a dinner I had with the Missonis, the fashion designers, at their house outside Milan. When the ten guests arrived, we were greeted by their children and grandchildren. Informal cocktails and hors d'oeuvres were served, then Mrs. Missoni took us to see her garden and showed us a stream where crawfish lived. We looked for four-leaf clovers and played with the children. Eventually, the children disappeared and then we were seated at a huge, informally elegant table. Everything was served family style, but the cooking and seasonings were perfect. It reflected their style. The spirit was casual but very elegant, just like their clothes. Just as one of the sweaters they've designed is extraordinarily comfortable yet suitable for the most elegant occasion."

When you're comfortable with what you're doing, your guests sense that and enjoy themselves more. "I once attended a small dinner party," Sheraton says, "given by people who obviously thought they had a lot of style, but everything they did that evening stood for something else.

"There was supermarket dyed lumpfish caviar, served in a great big crock of ice surrounded by toast, as though it were caviar of the finest quality. The lumpfish caviar is the kind you should mix with cream cheese and serve as a spread. They served a canned ham studded with cloves, as though it were a real ham. They had frozen green beans instead of fresh. It felt as though they were saying 'we all know what this is supposed to be, but this is the best we can do.' It wasn't bad food, but they had gone to a lot of trouble and it was dull. Who wants phony-fancy? For half the effort, and probably half the price, they could have served real chili or real beef stew, and it would have been so much more interesting."

Being secure enough be comfortable with yourself and what you have, rather than being concerned with trappings, shows great style. You can do marvelous things with earthenware pottery and inexpensive flowers. They're just as pretty as china and expensive flowers.

"Many people are too timid to serve a simple meal, so they add too many spices and sauces to it. That's guilding the lily. It's like a lady who is perfectly dressed, then she adds pearls. Next, she says, 'oh, well, I have the pearls, I'll put on earrings.' And she adds more until she ruins her appearance. We all tend to do that; it's human nature. Too often we decide a simple thing cannot be accepted, it has to be gilded. And we have to be careful not to do that. In the appreciation of food, it's so very important."
—LUCIO SORRE, *Villa Banfi*

PLANNING A MEAL

"Unless I'm serving people I've eaten with many times," Mimi Sheraton says, "people that I know will eat anything, I won't serve stuffed calves' hearts, or innards, or liver, anything like that. There are a lot of people who don't like those dishes. I might ask guests that I don't know very well if there's anything they hate. A lot of people don't feel that way, they think that the guest should make do with what he's served, but I don't want to make a Greek stuffed eggplant and then find out that one of my guests hates eggplant, or is allergic to it. I want everyone to enjoy the meal I've prepared.

"I believe that if someone is asked to dinner, they should mention any food allergies they have as soon as they're invited. I don't think they should just announce likes and dislikes unless they're asked, but if there's a health problem involved the guest should say 'look, I don't want to make this any special deal, but I just want you to know that I can't eat this,' or 'leave me out of that course.'"

You should be able to enjoy your own party as much as your guests will, so don't leave anything to the last minute. Decide if you want to cook and serve the food yourself, or if you'd rather have help. Hiring help for a dinner party is an individual choice—some people prefer to do without.

Even if you do hire help, take care of all the important details yourself. Check the cutlery and glassware you plan to use. Ideally, you should have a spare place setting or two to allow for a plate being broken at the last minute or a fork dropped on the floor during dinner. (A host shouldn't have to take the fork out and wash it during the meal, or give the guest a replacement fork that doesn't match the other cutlery.)

Don't ignore serving spoons—always put two or three more than you think you'll need on the table. "There are some very clumsy

people about—while they are talking, they let go of the vegetable spoon and it slides into the dish," according to British caterer Frank Hurd. "You don't want to fish it out; it's much better to leave it in and use another. And it's surprising how many people will take the spoon out of the peas and replace it in the beans, leaving one dish

"A great part of the pleasure in the art of good living is in savoring things. And savoring does not mean sending an interior decorater to work with the chef, as nouvelle cuisine does—the slivers of tulips and half a macaroon (to suggest the dark side of the moon) garnishing two emaciated shrimp floating in a slimy mass of cream. Open your eyes to food. Don't say 'now I'm really going to get into food' and go buy twenty different kinds of vegetables at once; try one new thing at a time, and savor each. Take your time."
—LUCIO SORRE, *Villa Banfi*

with two spoons in it and the other without any. You can't take a spoon out of the beans and put it back in the peas in front of a guest; you'll embarrass him. Instead, leave two spoons in the beans and provide a clean spoon for the peas."

●

Once you've chosen and counted your glassware and cutlery, polish the glass until it shines. This really doesn't take very long, and it makes all the difference in the appearance of the finished table.

TO POLISH A PLATE

1. Hold the plate in both hands with a tea towel. The plate should be facing you, with your fingers spread out on the back of the plate and both thumbs holding the towel against the front of the rim.
2. Turn the plate by bringing your right hand up to your left, then your left hand down to your right. The plate will turn counterclockwise.

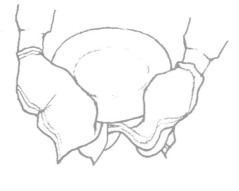

3. The rim is now polished. To polish its front and back, hold the plate firmly in your right hand and the tea towel in your left. Rub the front and back with the towel using brisk, circular motions. After a few seconds, hold the plate up to the light to check for marks. There shouldn't be any but if there are, rub it again.

TO POLISH A GLASS

1. With a tea towel spread across both hands, pick up the glass. Insert part of the cloth into the bowl and turn the glass upside down so it rests in your right hand with your towel-covered thumb in its bowl and your fingers resting loosely against the outside of the towel-covered bowl. Support its upturned bottom, also covered with cloth, with your left hand.

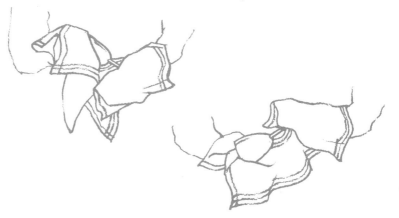

2. Turn the glass clockwise with your right hand. (You can turn your left hand counterclockwise to help it along.)
3. Rotate it gently two or three complete turns to bring up a brilliant shine.

Once you've finished polishing, touch the glass only with hands that are covered by a clean towel to avoid leaving fingerprints.

To polish silver, you'll need two soft cloths and nonabrasive commercial liquid polish. Fold one of the cloths two or three times —this will be used to apply the polish. The other cloth is for buffing the silver to bring up its shine. For an unsurpassed shine, finish up by buffing the silver with a chamois cloth.

Once the glassware and silver is polished, you're almost ready to set the table. Arrange the chairs around the table first so that you can line up the place settings properly. Chairs should be placed directly opposite one another with a comfortable amount of space between each so your guests won't feel crowded. Make sure that you seat compatible guests together to encourage conversation.

TO SET THE TABLE

Even if you entertain only occasionally, consider investing in a good linen tablecloth and napkins. They'll last for decades and are unbeatable for giving a table an elegant appearance.

"The food is the star," says Geoffrey Beene, "so I have white linen placemats, white napkins, and white Wedgwood plates, so there's absolutely no distraction. The table is as simple and clean-looking as possible, so the food stands out."

Mimi Sheraton prefers a more lively, but equally correct, table setting. "I myself don't like the formal settings of white damask cloth or old pastels. Most of my china is white, and I prefer to put it against strong, bright colors and patterns. I also think it's a good idea to carry the color scheme of the dining room through to the table setting."

When buying any tablecloth, remember that it should be long enough to fall approximately halfway to the floor, and its center crease should be aligned with the center of your table. Once your tablecloth is on the table, add the centerpiece.

You can use your imagination here and make almost anything you like a focal point of your table, but fresh fruit or an appealing arrangement of fresh flowers are reliable standbys. If you're using an arrangement of fruit, treat it as you would glassware and cutlery—polish it until it's glossy with a fresh towel or napkin, then place it in its bowl and don't touch it again.

If you're using candles, place them on either side of the centerpiece or at each corner of the table.

"Nothing is more pleasant than the tie of host and guest."
—AESCHYLUS

As you set the table, always keep your guests' comfort and convenience in mind. No one should have to reach across the table for salt, pepper, or other condiments, nor should they have to constantly interrupt the conversation by asking other diners to pass things to them. Condiments should be placed between every two place settings for easy access. Never put bottled sauces on the table—take an extra minute and transfer them to sauceboats.

Arrange cutlery next to the plates in the order in which they'll be used, working from the outside in. Knives and spoons should always be on the right; forks should always be on the left.

Glasses should be to the right of the plate, slightly above the dinner knife. Glasses should be arranged from front to back in the order of their use. Place a separate glass for each type of wine you'll be serving, with a water goblet behind and to the left of them. If you're offering champagne as well, you can either place the champagne glass behind the wineglasses or bring out the champagne glasses after the wineglasses have been removed.

GLASSWARE

A good wine glass is of a size and shape that complements the bouquet and flavor of the wine. The top edge of the glass should curve in slightly to hold the bouquet. Its stem should be sturdy enough not to snap if held firmly, and long enough to keep the heat of your hand from traveling quickly to the bowl of the glass and warming the wine. When filled to the brim, the glass should hold between seven and nine ounces of liquid, so it will hold a generous serving when properly half-filled with wine. It should also be crystal-clear, to allow you to inspect and enjoy the color of the wine. And, finally, remember that wine glasses will get broken, so you should always have a few more than you think you'll need.

TYPES OF WINEGLASSES

The *all-purpose wine glass* has a long stem, convex rim, and an eight- to ten-ounce capacity. It is appropriate (although not necessarily ideal) for any wine and any table setting.

The *tulip glass for red wine* is traditional for serving strong red table wines from France, Italy, Spain, and California. Its distinctive shape was created by Viennese glass blowers in the sixteenth century.

The *Paris goblet* is best suited to full-bodied reds such as the wines of Burgundy and Bordeaux, and their international counterparts. Its strongly curved rim holds the wine's bouquet, and the rounded bowl allows the proper amount of hand warmth to reach the wine and open its flavor.

The *white wine glass* is smaller than the standard red wine glass, usually with a maximum capacity of eight ounces. (The smaller size is appropriate because white wines, with their high levels of acidity, are best tasted in small amounts.) Its elongated stem protects the bowl from hand warmth.

The *copita*, or "little cup" (four to five ounces) is ideal for Sherry, Port, and Madeira.

The *tulip glass for Champagne* is the best choice for maximizing the drink's bouquet and bubbles. Other types of Champagne glasses—the shallow, broad rimmed *coupe* and the straight-sided *flute*—don't show Champagne off to its best advantage. (The flute is perhaps the best choice for beer.)

WASHING GLASSES

The key to washing any glass item, but especially wine glasses, is proper rinsing. Without thorough rinsing, a dull soap film will dry on the glass and detract from its luster. To rinse wineglasses, pour warm water into each glass, letting it spill over the rim. Leave a little bit of warm water in the bottom of each glass as you remove them from the sink, because warm glasses are easier to dry and polish than cold ones.

"A hearty dish like a cassoulet or a stew needs a wine with the brashness of youth; a wine with a lot of taste, acidity, and sharpness to it to blend with the food. If you serve a sedate or well-matured red wine, the wine will seem like a man in a three-piece-suit in a disco. It will not fit."
—LUCIO SORRE, *Villa Banfi*

FOOD AND WINE

The matching of food and wine is a matter of personal taste and selection. The goal is to join foods and wines that complement each other so that neither dominates. This means simply that a delicate food will be most enjoyed if served with a delicate wine. And the converse: a sturdy roast, for example, can be best served with a "sturdy" or big red wine. The final combinations are yours to make.

SERVING WINE

Although most ordinary table wines are ready to drink when you buy them, they benefit from a few days—or at least a few hours—of laying down and settling before you uncork them. Wines that mature quickly—Beaujolais, most sweet or dry white wines, and rosés—should never be kept for more than three years after their bottling date or the wine will begin to break down.

The classic red wines—vintage Burgundies and Bordeaux, Italian reds, and some California vintage-bottled varietals—need time to reach their full flavor. Ask a trusted wine retailer about the time necessary for laying down these wines before serving.

A good wine merchant is important to any wine buyer. Try to find a wine shop where the staff doesn't only sell wines but also knows and appreciates them. Sample a few shops, and ask questions. Do the sales people have time to explain things to you? If not, go elsewhere. If the merchant simply hands you a bottle and says "this is good," try someplace else. Ideally, a wine merchant will ask questions of his own. "What are you serving with the wine? How many guests are you having?" And then he'll offer his suggestions.

STORING WINE

Ideally, wines should be kept at a constant temperature, but that isn't a realistic option in most homes. According to London wine collector Christopher Selmes, you "need not worry, if the house or apartment is air-conditioned and the temperature isn't going up into the nineties. The only real enemies are wild temperature fluctuation and excessive direct light." A wine will keep well for at least a year under these conditions. If you're planning to keep an expensive wine for more than a year or so, you should have it professionally stored in a retailer's cellar or warehouse or in a privately rented wine locker in an air-conditioned commercial warehouse.

GRAPE VARIETIES

BARBERA:
Grown primarily in the Piedmont region of Italy, this grape produces a fine, robust red wine. There is also a California barbera, which produces a dry, fruity table wine.

CABERNET SAUVIGNON
The most important ingredient in the renowned clarets of France's Bordeaux region, this grape is also often blended with other grape varieties to produce some of the finest wines of California, Argentina, Australia, and eastern Europe.

If you're really interested in developing your own "wine cellar," you can install a cooling unit in a closet or other available space. Self-contained wine lockers range in price from $1,000 to $5,000.

Nearly all wines should be stored horizontally, or as near to horizontal as possible. (Jug wines and fortified wines—Port, Sherry, Madeira and brandy—are the exceptions to the rule.) The neck can be angled slightly up or down, as long as the wine in the bottle touches the base of the cork to keep air from entering the bottle. Champagne in particular should never be stored upright for more than a few weeks, as it will turn flat.

You can choose from a variety of inexpensive racks to store and display your wine collection. Make sure that you place the rack in a vibration-free area. You can check this by placing a filled wineglass on the floor of your storage area. If concentric rings or ripples appear on the liquid's surface, find another storage area. And always keep wine racks away from kitchen appliances—refrigerators and dishwashers are notorious for creating vibrations.

SERVING TEMPERATURES

Generally, the sweeter a wine, the cooler its serving temperature. Although the phrase "room temperature" is often used, don't take it too literally. Practically speaking, "room temperature" refers to a range between 60°F and 65°F that is considered ideal for domestic burgundies, zinfandels, the red wines of Burgundy, the Rhône, Bordeaux, and the Loire, chianti, barolo, grignolino, Port, Madeira, Marsala, and muscatel. To see if a bottle falls into this temperature range, touch it with your hand. If it feels cool but not cold, it's the proper serving temperature. If it feels warm, five to ten minutes in the refrigerator followed by two to three minutes out of the refrigerator should bring it to the proper temperature. Other wines:

Sweet white wines: 40 to 45°F

Semi-sweet wines: 45 to 50°F

Dry white wines: 46 to 52°F

Young red wines: 48 to 52°F

Dry rosés: 46 to 52°F

Semi-sweet rosés: 45 to 50°F

Sparkling wines/Champagne: 40 to 45°F

CHILLING WINE

The most elegant and effective method of chilling wine is in an ice bucket. Fill the bucket with one third cold water to two thirds ice and immerse the bottle in the mixture up to its shoulder. Ten minutes in the bucket equals and hour in the refrigerator.

UNCORKING A BOTTLE

Opening a wine bottle is easiest when you have the proper tools. The screw portion of a corkscrew should be hollow, slightly flattened steel about two and a half inches long (a hollow screw can grasp the inside of the cork firmly to minimize breakage). Professional wine stewards usually use a wine butler's tool consisting of a corkscrew, a sharp blade to cut bottle neck capsules and wires, and a bottle cap remover. Pronged cork extractors are also available for removing corks stuck in bottle necks.

You can remove a cork in four steps using a wine butler's tool.

1. Use the small blade to cut the seal that covers the cork and remove the upper part of the capsule. Wipe the cork and the bottle's lip and neck with a clean cloth.

2. Place the tip of the screw slightly to the side of the cork's center and gently turn it into the cork until it is about a quarter-inch from the base of the cork. (If it pierces the bottom of the cork, fragments will fall into the wine.)

3. Place the inside edge of the lever against the edge of the bottle neck and draw the cork up by raising the handle of the tool.

4. When the cork is nearly free of the bottle neck, remove the corkscrew and use your fingers to gently force it the rest of the way out.

LETTING WINE BREATHE

Wine needs controlled contact with oxygen to attain its full flavor and become "soft." White wine, rosés, and non-complex reds, such as Beaujolais, need to breathe for only five to fifteen minutes; sturdier red wines always need more time than that. The younger a red wine, the more breathing time it needs to reach drinking softness. Old, fine reds may be ruined if allowed to breathe too long. To guage the time required for an older wine, taste the wine as soon as it is uncorked. If it seems rough, the wine needs about twenty minutes to breathe. If the taste seems perfect, go ahead and pour.

TO TASTE A WINE

First, you need a glass that's comfortable, with about a six- or eight-ounce capacity, stemmed, and crystal clear—no designs, no color. Fill approximately one-third of the glass with wine, and look at its color against a naked light—an incandescent light bulb or a candle. You cannot properly evaluate color against a flourescent light because the flourescent light washes out the color.

The wine should be crystal clear, without any matter in suspension. A dry white wine should be free of brownish tint, which would indicate that the wine is going over the edge. Its color should range from very pale to an amber. The darker, more intense its color, the more body the wine will have. "Body" means simply that when you take a sip, your mouth will be filled by its taste.

When viewing a red wine, the rule of thumb is: the brighter the color, the younger the wine. If you see a brownish color, a rusty color, or a brick-colored tint, the wine is aged, which is desirable. A red wine always needs to age a bit.

Then take the wine glass by the stem and swirl it. Swirling the wine brings it into contact with the air. As the liquid reacts with the oxygen, certain alcohols in the wine (called esters) are released. After you've swirled the glass and the esters have been released, sniff the wine. Do this by putting your nose as close to the wine as possible. You're trying to detect the faint scent of the grape. If the wine smells very grapey, you may say it is very young. That is known as an aroma. If it smells faintly grapey and has a pleasant scent, that is known as a bouquet—an aroma that has undergone some changes and development in the bottle through aging. What you don't want to smell is mustiness, or any foreign odors. If the wine's bouquet is acceptable, then you're ready to taste.

In general, white wines should always be drunk young (some younger than others, depending on the complexity of the wine) and most red wine can stand up to aging. However, all wine has a lifespan. It does not last forever. And while it is very interesting, even rather charming, to see people paying thousands of dollars for bottles of wine that have been in the cellar for 50, 70, 100, 200 years, all that's inside those bottles are memories. The wine is far beyond its peak.

To taste, take a small amount of wine and swirl it under and over the tongue and all around the mouth. By rinsing your mouth with the wine, the wine will come in contact with all the parts of your mouth, and each part reacts to the various components of the wine. The tip of your tongue senses its sweetness, the tip and the edges of your tongue sense its saltiness, and the back of the tongue senses its bitterness. Bitterness is always a poor word, but there is no better one—the sensation is sometimes referred to as an "almond-like quality." What you are looking for is first a sensation of a touch of sweetness, mitigated by some astringency on the walls of your mouth. Next, if you are going to taste professionally, exhale through your nose while the wine is still in your mouth. This gives you a sense of what the wine would taste like if you were to swallow.

CHARDONNAY/PINOT CHARDONNAY

One of the finest of all white grape varieties, the chardonnay is the primary white grape of burgundy and chablis.

CHENIN BLANC

A native of the Loire Valley in France, this grape produces white wines that can range from dry to flowery to fruity. The American chenin blanc grape produces a light, dry table wine with a fruity flavor and aroma.

GAMAY

An essential component of the wines of France's Beajolais region, this grape is also grown in California. A wine made from gamay grapes should be fruity, tart, and spicy.

After the wine is gone from your mouth, whether you swallow it or spit it out, what remains is called the aftertaste—the memory of the wine. And if the wine is very light, very young, that memory will last a short time. If the wine is more complex, it will last longer. The longer the wine taste lingers, the more complex, the more full-bodied, the more important the wine is.

What you don't want to taste—and it sometimes happens—is a burst of fruit and the promise of a lot of taste followed by nothing. As the wine reaches the middle of your mouth, there is no taste. It falls down. If the wine is very young, it simply may not be developed enough. If it isn't very young, it may be poorly made. Experience tells you which is which.

You may occasionally taste a young wine that hasn't matured. You'll taste the fruit and the first sensation of sweetness, but then you may feel different sensations in your mouth that do not knit together. Those sensations indicate that the wine is still forming, still building up. There's nothing wrong with it, it's a young wine that in a year or two or three may become excellent.

With a red wine, you will sometimes feel a puckering sensation on the walls of the mouth. That's tannic acid, the same tannic acid that you detect if you eat a green apple. As the wine ages in the bottle, the tannin slowly disappears and becomes "softness"—the sensation you feel in your mouth when there are no sharp edges, just a delicate feeling of roundness. So when a wine is big and soft, it means that it fills your mouth with taste and there are no sharp edges, just nice soft roundness.

In essence, if the wine pleases you, if there's nothing strange about it, then it's a good wine. You may not like a certain taste—that's your own personal reaction to the wine. But a well-made wine will be fairly well-balanced, will have a touch of sweetness when you taste it, may be more or less dry, and will be pleasant even though you may not like the taste.

GRENACHE

Originally grown only in France's Rhône Valley, this grape has been exported to nearly all of the world's major wine-producing regions. It is used in the production of rosés and in blends of Châteauneuf-du-Pape.

LABRUSCA

A principal species of North American grape, cultivated primarily in New York and Washington states. Concord grapes are a typical example of the labrusca species.

LAMBRUSCO

A red wine grape from Italy, the lambrusco produces slightly sparkling wines that are often surprisingly dry.

MERLOT

A secondary grape of Bordeaux used in the blending of the great clarets, its primary purpose is to the soften the flavor of harsher grapes, such as the cabernet sauvignon. An American merlot wine is aromatic and spicy.

NEBBIOLO

Native to Italy's Piedmont region, this grape is responsible for that country's greatest red wines.

Overall, you're looking for wine that is balanced. You want to see a pleasant, clear color. You want to smell a fruity bouquet—the scent of the grape, more or less pronounced. The taste should carry over, so that what you detect at the top of the tongue becomes rich as the wine reaches the back of the tongue and goes down. That richness should carry over—it should linger on for a few seconds after you've swallowed the wine. That's a well-balanced wine. Not one characteristic stands out.

TASTING NOTES

A number of taboos are recognized by professional wine experts when tasting wines. Of course, it's not possible to pay attention to all of them when drinking wine in a social situation, but the guidelines are worth noting. Because strong odors interfere with the olfactory tonalities of wine, smoking is frowned upon before or during a pure tasting. Men should not wear shaving lotion or cologne, and women should not wear perfume or lipstick. (If a woman wearing lipstick tastes a sparkling wine or Champagne, the wine will go flat in the glass.)

There are some foods that adversely affect the taste of wine. If, for instance, you drink wine with an egg dish, or with a cream sauce containing eggs, the wine will taste of sulfur. Artichokes, fennel, and asparagus flatten out the taste of wine, making it taste like water. And you should avoid eating anything containing vinegar if you want to highlight a wine—pickles or peppers or salad dressing containing vinegar should be avoided. You can minimize the problem with salad by using lemon juice in the dressing instead of vinegar, but the wine will still taste a bit less than its best. The taste of white wine is more easily affected that that of the sturdier, fuller-bodied reds.

DECANTING WINE

Decanting wine—transferring it from its original bottle to a decanter—aerates the wine, freeing it to begin the process of opening up to its fullest flavor. It also allows you to separate the wine from

PINOT NOIR
Native to Burgundy, this grape produces some of the world's noblest red wines and is also a component of great champagnes. It has been successfully cultivated in California, but the climate there prevents them from achieving the greatness they attain in France.

RIESLING
A component of nearly all of Germany's finest wines, this grape is native to the Rhine and Moselle valleys. It is also grown in the United States, Australia, and other wine-producing regions. A California riesling should be straw-colored with a fruity aroma.

SAUVIGNON BLANC/FUMÉ BLANC
Native to Bordeaux, this grape produces white wines that range from dry to sweet.

SEMILLION
The primary grape of the great dessert wines of Sauternes, France. The California semillion produces sweet domestic wines as well as some drier varieties.

any sediment that may be suspended in the wine, giving it an unpleasant appearance and a grainy, bitter taste. Decanting a red wine into a clear glass container lets you see its true color, which is normally masked by the light-resistant tinted bottles that usually hold red wines.

Generally, the only wines that shouldn't be decanted are whites, rosés, and Champagnes. Since these wines should remain properly chilled, they're best kept in an ice bucket rather than a decanter.

Decanters themselves range from etched-crystal vessels to humble water pitchers. It's important only that any container used is made of clear glass and is thoroughly clean (but never smelling of detergent).

Decanting calls for patience and a steady arm. Ideally, you'll have a strong light from either an incandescent bulb or a candle behind the wine bottle, making it possible to see the sediment clearly. Hold the opened bottle in one hand, being careful not to stir the sediment. Hold the decanter in your other hand. With one continuous movement, pour the wine slowly into the decanter, allowing it to come in contact with the neck of the decanter. (If the wine drops directly onto the bottom of the decanter, it's being deprived of necessary contact with the air.) Keep a close eye on the bottle—when sediment rises to the neck of the bottle, stop pouring. If you've decanted properly, only about half an inch of wine will remain in the original bottle. Even this can be rescued—just stand the bottle upright and, at the end of the meal, pour out the clear remainder. The sediment should stay behind.

When decanting old ports or Madeiras, use a fine-meshed wine sieve to strain out crusty particles. When decanting any light red wine less than three years old, it's not necessary to provide a light, but the other rules apply.

If you choose to serve wine from a decanter, make sure that it sparkles like the rest of your table. Frank Hurd recalls the butler's

SYLVANER
Grown in Germany, Alsace, California, and other wine-producing regions, this grapes produces light-bodied, undistinguished white wines. The American sylvaner is sometimes called the Franken Riesling.

TREBBIANO
The primary grape of central Italy, this grape produces Orvieto, Soave, and Chianti.

ZINFANDEL
The most widely cultivated red grape variety in California, this grape makes full-bodied wines of varied character. Its exact origins are unknown, but there are some indications that it may be the Primitvo from the Bari region of Italy.

method of cleaning a decanter: "Butlers traditionally clean a decanter with water containing salt and shot from a cartridge. Fill the decanter with half a pint of warm water and add a couple of teaspoons of salt and the shot from a cartridge. Grasp the neck of the decanter with your right hand and support its base with your left hand. Swirl the mixture around inside the decanter until the sediment pulls away from the sides and base. Pour the mixture into a sieve to save the shot. Then wash the inside of the decanter with a little detergent and warm water. Again holding the decanter firmly at the neck, swish the detergent mixture around the decanter, then empty it.

"Make sure you rinse the decanter well two or three times. For the last rinse, fill it one-third full of warm water and empty it. Briskly dry the outside of the decanter with a tea towel, then turn it upside down and shake it to empty drop of water from the inside. Make sure you hold it securely as you shake it—decanters tend to be heavy and awkward, and can easily crash to the floor if you're not careful."

To serve from a decanter, hold it firmly around the neck just underneath the lip so it can be easily poured. If you'd rather offer your guests a choice of two different wines, try the butler's technique for serving from two bottles at once.

Hold the bottle you think will be less popular in your left hand (you'll be serving from the right, so it will be more awkward to pour from the bottle held in your left hand). To pour with your right hand, you need only bend your wrist toward the glass. To pour with your left hand, you'll need to bend your wrist backward toward the glass.

If you want to serve one wine from a bottle and a second from a decanter, hold the decanter in your right hand, because it is awkwardly shaped and more difficult to pour. A wineglass should be two-thirds full—never more than that.

SERVING FOOD

There's no mystery to serving your guests properly and efficiently. Just remember that food is always served from the left; drinks are always served from the right. If you're going around the table placing plates in front of your guests, hold the stack of plates in your right hand so you can place each one down smoothly with your left.

When offering a serving dish for your guests to help themselves, you'll be most comfortable if you stand to your guest's left and place your left foot one step in front of your right to help you keep your balance. Flexing your left knee, bend from the waist and bend your left elbow to bring the dish within easy reach of your guest. Make sure it's near enough to his plate to allow him to serve himself without dropping food to the table. (Take care not to thrust it too near his chin—you'll make him nervous, and holding a dish that high will tire your arms quickly.)

BEING SERVED

At a dinner party, you and your fellow guests will be more comfortable if you help yourself to the various dishes properly.

Serving utensils are placed for the convenience of the person being served, and they should be replaced in the same position. The spoon and fork should be together on the left-hand side of the dish, with the spoon to the right of the fork.

After helping yourself to pâté or cheese, replace the knife so that the handle faces toward you. When taking gravy or sauce from a sauceboat, replace the ladle over the lip, not over the side, to keep the sauceboat balanced.

TO FOLD A NAPKIN

A properly folded linen napkin makes a striking impression with any table setting. There are several types of folds to choose from, and each one can be easily learned and quickly executed.

All napkin folds begin with a well-pressed twenty-four to twenty-six-inch-across napkin.

The Plain Fold is the beginning of more elaborate folds, or it can be left alone for a stark, simple look.

1. Lay the napkin flat on the table.

2. Fold down the top third of the napkin.

3. Turn the napkin over so that the fold is toward you.

4. Bring the bottom edge of the napkin up even with the top.

5. Fold its left edge in to the center.

6. Turn the napkin over, keeping the fold on the left side.

7. Fold the left edge to the center again.

8. Turn the napkin over again, still keeping the fold on the left side.

9. Fold the napkin in half, forming a rectangle. Press the napkin lightly to keep its folds crisp.

The Lazy Footman

1. Lay the plainly folded napkin on the table.

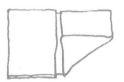

2. Open the last fold. If the center crease is visible, turn the napkin over.

3. Bring the lower right-hand corner to the center, creating a small triangle.

4. Bring the lower left-hand corner to the center, creating a small triangle.

5. Turn the napkin over so that the center crease is visible. The napkin should now look like a large triangle, with its base closest to you.

6. Pick up the napkin and insert the right end into the corner of the left end.

7. Turn the napkin top to bottom. There should be a fold at its back where the two ends of the base are tucked into one another.

8. Stand the napkin on its base. If it looks very stiff, soften it by gently tapping the front.

AFTER THE PARTY

Cleaning up is always a chore, but you can make it easier. And proper cleaning and storage ensures that your glassware and cutlery will be in top condition the next time you need them.

Naturally a dishwasher makes the cleanup easier, but remember that delicate glasses or china should be washed by hand to protect them. Silverware should also be hand-washed, as a machine will easily scratch it. In the long run, it's best to leave your guests alone for a few minutes between courses so that you can wash each set of dishes. It shouldn't take long, and you'll be glad not to have to face the mess created by leaving the dishes from the entire meal. However, if you're not comfortable leaving your guests, don't hurry through the cleanup—you'll probably break something. Instead, simply scrape the leftover food from the plates and stack them neatly by the sink until the meal is finished.

If you have stragglers—guests who seem to have no intention of ever going home—the most you can do is hint that it's time to go. Try mentioning your early morning meeting, or the fact that they have to be at work the next morning. Eventually, they'll catch on. "I've seen some hosts use a great ploy to end long goodbyes," says executive recruiter James Hunt. "The host will shake the guest's hand, and before the guest knows it he's been pulled out the door."

Never let an intoxicated guest drive home. Instead, find him a ride or call a taxi and prepay the driver. You're not only protecting your friend and other drivers—in some states, you can be held responsible for damage done by a drunken guest who tries to drive. Your guest may be embarrassed or even angry the next morning, but that's a small price to pay for protecting him and yourself.

CATERING

You can have a party in your home with none of the cooking or cleaning-up headaches if you call in a caterer.

"I don't think everybody has to know how to cook, or has to cook well," says Mimi Sheraton. "There are a lot of people who would like to have people to dinner but are simply not interested in cooking. And they don't have to be. They'll be just as well off buying food, with some planning and originality."

Jean-Claude Nédélec and Sean Driscoll own Glorious Food, a complete catering service with offices in New York and Washington, D.C. The company is famed for its superior food and meticulous planning and service and often caters social functions held at various museums, including New York City's Metropolitan Museum of Art and Museum of Modern Art. Glorious Food handled the president's inaugural luncheon in 1985. They manage to make a party as enjoyable for the host as it is for his guests.

"Some caterers will just drop off a platter," Nédélec says. "We don't do that. We like to have clients tell us as much as they possibly can about the type of party they're having and what they'd like to serve, and then let us handle everything.

"When a client first contacts us, if we've never worked with him before, an account executive will visit his home to check the layout. The exective will look at the kitchen to see what kinds of dishes can and cannot be prepared there, and then he'll sit down with the client to discuss the type of event it's going to be. Then we'll send the client several menus, and he can choose the dishes that appeal to him from each one. We'll also provide a proposal that lists the estimate costs of the party.

"Our services are not inexpensive," Nédélec explains. "In addition to the the food, we charge for the services of the chefs, butlers, and bartenders. And we can provide tables, chairs, tablecloths, trays, plates, glasses, and flatware but those rental items carry an extra charge. The service and rental charges together can equal the cost of the food. We don't provide liquor—instead, we'll suggest to the client exactly what he should buy to complement the food he's

"We like clients to tell us what they want, then stand back and let us take care of everything. Nobody's going to pretend that they're not having the affair catered, or that the caterer's staff is really their own household staff, but it's perfectly okay for them to tell us they'd like to keep everything as homey as possible. Some people don't want fancy food—they prefer chicken pot pie and apple tarts. We have absolutely no objections to serving plain food, with a minimum of fuss."
—JEAN-CLAUDE NÉDÉLEC,
Glorious Food

chosen and order it from the liquor store for him. The liquor store will then bill the client directly.

"We don't dictate to clients, but once the decisions are made we like to be able to take over. When we arrive at a house, we take over the whole kitchen. We don't want to see anybody else in there, except perhaps the client's maid or a person who does the dishes. It's not that we don't want anyone to see what we're doing, but if you have three or four people constantly underfoot, chances are somebody's going to crash into our things. And that's annoying."

Nédélec's butlers, who may be called on to tend bar, serve hors d'oeuvres, perform a formal dinner service, set tables, clean up afterward, and even occasionally arrange flowers, are skilled at their work. "We have about thirty who work constantly for us," he says, "and close to 900 more who freelance for us. They're mostly actors, students, dancers, people who want to be in the performing arts.

"The butlers will usually arrive at the client's home about two hours before the guests will, and begin setting up. The chefs and kitchen workers arrive about an hour before the party and begin cooking. We prepare the food in our kitchens, but we prefer to do as much cooking as possible at the last minute, in the client's kitchen. That's no problem at a dinner for thirty to forty people in most private homes."

Nédélec suggests you contact a caterer well in advance of your planned party. "During the slow season," he says, "from January through March, a few days' notice may be enough, but two to three weeks' notice is sufficient for the average dinner at even the busiest time of year."

The services of Glorious Food may be more extensive than you need, but there are acceptable alternatives.

"If you don't want to use a full-service caterer," says Mimi Sheraton, "you can go to a take-out store or find someone who will cook the food and send it over to you. This is much better than struggling to make a meal that's going to be terrible. If you don't enjoy cooking, forcing yourself to cook for guests will almost always have unsatisfactory results. You can show your guests that you care by taking pains to arrange and present the food attractively."

BEING A GUEST

Since his profession demands that he attend many receptions and parties, Alan Parter has become a skilled guest.

"Even if I don't know anyone there," he says, "I feel no compunction about going up to people and starting to ask them questions. I like to learn, and I enjoy listening to people. I've noticed that I'm never the only person who's alone at a reception, there are always at least a few others, and they appreciate the company.

"I've learned that if you're going to receptions, you have to work them," he explains. " 'Working' doesn't mean you can't have fun, but it does mean you have to make an effort to circulate, to build social and business relationships. I always try to remember the last time I met somebody, and make some reference to it in the conversation. I like nothing better than running into somebody I haven't seen in a year and saying 'Is your daughter still riding horses?' or 'How was that trip to the Virgin Islands?' Their faces just light up, because they want to talk about it and they appreciate the fact that you remember them and what they told you. It also works particularly well for me because I don't have a good memory for names, but I do remember conversations. I'm careful to always introduce myself by name in a social situation, even if the person might well know my name, because I know how comfortable it makes me when other people do that. It saves them embarrassment, in case they've forgotten."

Carlton Thompson finds that receptions are a valuable way to make and maintain business contacts. "I try to arrive on time," he says, "because then I can watch people arrive and see who I'd like to talk to. If you're late, most of the guests are hidden in the crowd. I just want to make contact, not have a meaningful business conversation, because you can't do that at a cocktail party. But you can be introduced to someone, and telephone his office later that week."

People who attend parties frequently, especially business-related parties, share a common problem—terminating a boring or unproductive conversation.

"I ask a lot of questions when I first meet someone. It's fun to find out what people do. You meet people who do interesting things that you know nothing about, and you learn from them. At the same time, you put them at ease since most people like to talk about themselves."
—JAMES HUNT,
Kenny, Kindler and Hunt

"The most difficult thing to learn was ending a conversation at a party," notes Parter. "I always want to be sensitive to other people's feelings, and one of the ways of showing that sensitivity is not embarrassing people. But most people are likely to be embarrassed if they feel that you're leaving them because they've been boring. In fact, you may want to end the conversation for a variety of reasons, but there's always the danger that you will be misinterpreted.

"Depending on the circumstances, I may tell the person that I want to go freshen my drink, or go to the men's room. Even if he realizes that I'm telling a little white lie, there's no reason for him to be personally offended. Or, very often, I will say, 'It's important for me to speak with some other people in the room, and I'm sure it is for you, too. I've really glad to have met you.' Even if you suspect you may have hurt him slightly, you can't worry about it. There's no point in standing around talking all evening with someone who doesn't interest you at all."

James Hunt agrees that it's always awkward to excuse yourself from a dull conversation with a fellow guest, but he's found an effective way of doing it with a minimum of embarrassment. "I usually say, 'Gee, that's interesting. Let me introduce you to so-and-so, I'm sure he would like to to hear about that too,'" he says. "Once the new person is added to the conversation, you can excuse yourself."

If a reception or cocktail party really doesn't interest you, you can properly leave afer a minimum of ten minutes. As Parter explains, "at most receptions, the host simply wants to see you there. He appreciates the fact that you respect him and his reception enough to put in an appearance. You may leave quickly and not even have time to speak with him, but he'll know that you were there. I will not be embarrassed to walk out after ten minutes, because I have shown my respect by going."

Although being a good guest is easier than being a host, there are still guidelines to follow to help make your host's job easier and to ensure that you and the other guests have a good time.

First, and perhaps most important, respond to invitations promptly and accurately. It is almost unforgivably rude to ignore an invitation completely, tell your host that you'll attend and then not show up, or tell your host that you can't attend and then appear at the party. (Of course, emergencies can force you to cancel out of a party unexpectedly, but this should be a very rare occurrence.)

It's not always a good idea to be "fashionably late." If the host is a good friend, you should arrive promptly—about ten minutes after the time stated on the invitation. He'll be glad to see you, and you'll have a chance to admire the preparations he's made for the party, something you won't be able to do once the crowd arrives.

If you do want to arrive late, make sure you understand the sort of party it is. If it begins at eight for dinner at half past, you should arrive no later than eight-fifteen. Don't embarrass the host and yourself by turning up in the middle of dinner.

You can properly leave a dinner party forty-five minutes after everyone has finished eating. Remember that your hosts are glad to see you—and they'll be even happier to see you next time if you don't wear out your welcome this time. If an invitation says that the party ends at a specific time, leave. Ideally, the room should be cleared fifteen or twenty minutes after the party's official end.

It is essential to thank your hosts for their hospitality before you leave, even if the party is large and they're difficult to find. Don't simply vanish when their backs are turned.

Strictly speaking, you should send a thank-you note immediately following a dinner party or a weekend visit. Don't wait more than a week or so to write and mail it—your hosts would like to hear from you before the party has been forgotten. If you think it would be appropriate to express your thanks over the telephone, make sure you call within a couple of days.